CONFIDENT & EPIC

21 DECISIONS TO LIVING YOUR BEST LIFE

LUCY LIU

Podcast Host

The Lucy Liu Show

"Lucy Liu's book is a great guide to building true confidence as she shares these decision making tips to help you move forward in your journey. As someone who talks about confidence, this is another great resource to have by your side when building your confidence in business and life."

Sheena Yap Chan — Wall Street Journal Bestselling Author and Podcast Host of "The Tao Of Self Confidence," Keynote Speaker, and Consultant on Self-confidence and Leadership

"Real. Raw. Relatable. Lucy fearlessly lays bare her own struggles and vulnerabilities, inviting readers on an emotionally charged journey of self-discovery and growth. Through her candid and relatable anecdotes, Lucy inspires readers to confront their own inner shadows with newfound courage and compassion. This book is a powerful guide to embracing our imperfections, fears, and doubts which lead to profound personal transformation and genuine connections with others."

Lauren Smith — Business Strategist, Author, Mentor, Podcast Host of "Master Your Mind, Business and Life" and "Awaken Your Soul."

"I read a lot of self-help, inspirational pieces, but this one really stuck with me. It felt deeply personal and honest, while also offering helpful insights and actionable ways to make improvements in life!"

Sydney Owens — Founder and Owner of Chicken Scratch, LLC

"Life is but a series of decisions. Lucy Liu eloquently shares stories and perspectives to help you navigate the art of decision making by transforming your mindset and living your purpose. Step into your own transformative power and make better decisions, large and small, and begin living the life you are called to live by following Lucy's journey of overcoming fear to transform and step into her life purpose - to help you discover what you can do to live the life you've dreamed of."

Robyn Graham — Marketing and Lead Generation Strategist, Host of "The Robyn Graham Show," Author of "You, Me, and Anxiety"

DEDICATED TO ANNABELLE

Dear Daughter,

I'm blown away by how incredibly smart you are and how sharp your mind is. I'm thankful for how you recognize emotions and try to comfort me in those needed moments.

You, my sweet girl, are wise beyond your years, and I'm so excited because I know great things are in store for you.

Every day I wake up and wonder how I can be a better mom for you, to set the best example for you, so you can be the best version of yourself and live the most epic life you deserve.

Thank you for being my daughter and for being the sweetest angel that you are!

Mommy loves you to the moon and back and can't wait to witness your beautiful life journey.

Oozes of love, always 🩶

PREFACE

Hi there, beautiful souls!

I wrote this book for you because I know you are a no-BS type of person.

You started your business or line of work to live the life of your choosing. You are successful in what you do.

Not only are you committed and willing to do the work, but you also seek to learn and continue to rapidly accelerate along the path to your desired results.

Maybe you already have enough money to take care of basic needs. Maybe you already live in your dream house, travel when and where you want, drive your dream car, and regularly hit your goals. But, maybe, it still feels like something is missing.

You still have this inner desire to change something you know needs to be changed.

And I believe you will. I believe you can, even more than you believe in yourself.

Contemplating the past 40 years, I didn't have a specific turning point or sudden epiphany which changed the course of my life.

But at 40 years old, I truly believe it is these decisions I made over the years which got me to where I am today.

If anything I say inspires you to make a mindset shift or to better your life, please share by tagging me @mslucyliu and #confidentandepic.

PREFACE

CONTENTS

Contents

"In any moment of decision, the best thing you can do is the right thing, the next best thing is the wrong thing, and the worst thing you can do is nothing."

— *Theodore Roosevelt*

DECISION #1
Mindset Shift

The powerhouse of the human body is the brain, but its driver is the mind. The mind controls everything we do along with how we react to what life throws at us. It is a hidden truth most people shy away from until they eventually have an experience that changes everything. We can only achieve within the capacity of our mindset.

Mindset is a set of beliefs which shape how we make sense of the world and events happening around us. Our mindset influences how we think, feel, and behave in any given situation. However, our mindset changes from moment to moment as different occurrences shape us and influence our thoughts.

Psychologists believe the mindset can be characterized as one of two types: the fixed mindset and the growth mindset. If we have a fixed mindset, then we believe our abilities and how we see things are fixed and, therefore, cannot be changed. We may also believe our talents and intelligence alone help us achieve success, and effort is not required. On the other hand, if we have a growth mindset, then we believe our talents and abilities can be developed over time through effort, persistence, and sometimes special moments which help our mindset to shift.

Many years ago, I witnessed a life-changing event which did some damage to my mind. This experience made me see things differently, and it troubled me for many years. I witnessed the death of a helpless boy in a hole made of shallow water.

The little boy was right beside me when he fell into the hole—a hole so deep, he toppled right in and never came out. At the time, I had no idea what life and death really meant, but I learned on this particular day that water had the power to swallow someone. There was screaming, plenty of crying, and massive panic all around, and what began as a beautiful day at the reservoir quickly turned into a five-year-old's worst nightmare. The hole was too deep for anyone around to help him.

This experience changed my mindset, making me view water in a new light. It is so calm and peaceful, yet it can be so dangerous. Before, I used to look forward to my parents taking me to the beach, but my feelings changed after I witnessed the death of that boy. Water became an enemy, and I would do anything just to avoid coming close to it. But, life always finds a way to make you face your deepest fears, and when it does, you either conquer the fear or fall prey to it.

I never told anyone this story until I became confident enough to share my fears and open myself up to the world. The memories and details are immensely vague, but the feelings are deeply ingrained. For many years, I felt fearful of the clear water of pools, agitation toward the moving currents of the ocean, anxiety over lakes, trepidation for reservoirs, and even dismay at the thought of drinking water. I would feel a cold chill go down my spine whenever I set my eyes on any body of water, even a calm flowing water. I wondered how something so calm and peaceful could also be so dangerous. And I hated myself for it along the way.

The struggle intensified in high school because a pass on the school's swimming proficiency exam was required for graduation. It felt like a death sentence to me, but I did not dare miss that test for anything. I guess the fear of a bad future was stronger than my fear of death by water. I practiced for a whole month at my best friend's house for this daunting test, which I was only able to pass by swimming with my head out of the water. Treading water for three minutes and swimming laps with my head raised above the water left my neck strained; it most certainly messed with my back, and my lungs endured substantial pain to the point where I had trouble breathing for the rest of the day.

Sometimes in life, we need to do things that feel impossible just to get what we want. If I had had a choice between running up a mountain and passing the swimming test, then I guess I would have discovered the height of Mount Everest. I was greatly terrified at any sight of water to the extent I tried to avoid anything that might make me see it. But life always comes with a different plan from what we all want and wish for.

For over 30 years, I was never able to swim with my head underwater. But almost a year after becoming a life coach, I realized that if I was talking the talk, then I needed to walk the walk and overcome my own fear. One day when my daughter asked me to put my head down and swim under water with her, I did it. That moment changed my thinking and mindset around life and fears. I felt like a hero who had fought a thousand wars and conquered. I felt like a proud parent, for the love of my daughter was way stronger than my fear of water.

This was a revelation for me, and it cut across all aspects of life. It has always been a struggle, but my determination to show strength and commitment to my daughter was another level of flex. This lesson proves that we all need to overcome that one fear before we can come out stronger from every challenge or fear we face in the future. Mindset is the key to conquering anything. In my wildest dreams, I wouldn't have imagined myself swimming with my head under the water. But no matter the challenge you face in this life, no matter how terrifying that thing may be, your mindset is the determining factor between winning and being afraid to try.

JOURNAL PROMPT #1

I made a decision to shift my mindset. While mindset is a moment-to-moment shift, it only takes one decision to change our lives. *What is one belief you've been holding on to for way too long that you know it's time to let go? Let's make a decision to change that.*

_____

_____

_____

_____

_____

_____

_____

_____

_____

_____

_____

_____

"It's not enough to have lived. We should be determined to live for something."

—*Winston S. Churchill*

DECISION #2
Life Purpose

B esides swimming, my biggest fear was death.
Occasionally in class, I would doodle in my college-ruled notebook a cement headstone with the big letters R.I.P. on it. Grass crawled around the headstone, and the name was forever forgotten.

I'll never forget all those nights of insomnia, laying in darkness with cold chills running down my spine. My fear of death often led to anxiety and a sense of unease. Other times, I also experienced an increased heart rate, sweating, trembling, and shortness of breath when confronted with the idea of death.

For so many years, I dwelled on the idea of why I feared death. Could it be because I was scared to experience excruciating pain and suffering? I couldn't even imagine what patients dying from cancer or other terminal illnesses felt or how frightening it would be to face the end, for it to be so near.

Could it be that I hated the idea of not having control? Death remains something which we have absolutely no control over. I've always sought control over my life, but I know deep down that birth, aging, sickness, and death are four things in life which can never be controlled by the self. The idea that there is no way to avoid this risk gives me chills.

Thank God I can rule out the fear of eternal punishment. Regardless of my religious or spiritual beliefs, I don't believe I will be punished for what I did in this life. I take every action knowing I am in full alignment with the results of my actions leading me to a better place in the afterlife.

My eventual conclusion was that my fear was not actually death—it was the fear of the unknown and the notion of being nonexistent. Death is the ultimate unknown in life because no one in the history of humanity has survived it to tell us the reality of what happens after we take our last breaths.

But even more importantly, *I was not living my life's purpose.*

Feeling like you're not living your life's purpose can evoke a range of emotions and sensations, and the experience may vary from person to person. For me, this looked like a lack of fulfillment. I felt a persistent sense of emptiness and dissatisfaction despite my accomplishments. If we are disconnected from our life purpose, then we might feel like something important is missing or a general feeling of discontentment.

At several points in my life, I've felt stuck and stagnant, frustrated and restless. Only later did I learn those were all nagging signs that there is actually something more meaningful or significant I should be doing in this life.

I started to feel a desire for a deeper sense of meaning in life and a more profound impact on the world. I yearned for a greater sense of contribution, a feeling that my actions align with my values and passions.

Once I put two and two together, I realized this is why all the uncertainties of life were so scary. Not knowing your life purpose can create a sense of uncertainty about your direction and decision-making. You might feel unsure about which path to pursue, leading to confusion and indecisiveness.

Honest clarity lies in letting things go, stepping back, and holding space for the unknown, in being present with contentment and allowing time to pass slowly as a healing process. I eventually ceased visualizing the grave and started visualizing the joyful version of myself five years in the future. I reframed my fears. I told myself repeatedly that *fear* is nothing but "False Evidence Appearing Real." And, I shifted my focus from what happens after death to how I can make my life more meaningful.

It's important to remember that discovering and living our life purpose is a highly individualized and ongoing journey. If you're experiencing these feelings too, it might be helpful to explore your values, interests, and passions, as well as seek support from trusted individuals or professionals who can assist you in clarifying your purpose and finding a path which aligns with your most authentic self.

Discovering and aligning with your life purpose can be a transformative and fulfilling experience. When we feel connected to our life purpose, it becomes easy to ignite a renewed sense of motivation and enthusiasm to engage in our daily activities. This newfound motivation can make it feel easier to stay focused and committed to all your endeavors as you may experience a natural enthusiasm and eagerness to pursue your goals and engage in activities connected to your purpose.

Discovering my life purpose brought about a greater sense of joy and gratitude. I found myself appreciating all the opportunities and experiences coming my way. Living a meaningful life that feels aligned with who I am led to a sense of joy and gratitude.

Discovering my life purpose brought with it a newfound clarity and focus. I now have a clear sense of direction and a deeper understanding of what truly matters to me. This allows me to make quick decisions and set goals with greater confidence and conviction.

Of course, the experience of living our purpose may evolve and change over time as we age, and it's natural to encounter challenges along the way. Our purpose acts as a guiding light during those challenging times, providing us with a sense of resilience and the motivation to overcome these obstacles. However, embracing and actively pursuing our life purpose can bring a sense of profound satisfaction and a deeper connection to ourselves and the world.

I am now living in accordance with my true self and expressing my unique talents, strengths, and values. This congruence between who I am and what I do have created a deep sense of congruence and inner harmony.

JOURNAL PROMPT #2

I made a decision to always live my life's purpose over all my fears. *Are you living your life's purpose? What is one fear you decide to let go of this year?*

_____

_____

_____

_____

_____

_____

_____

_____

_____

_____

_____

_____

_____

"Be yourself; everyone else is already taken."

— *Oscar Wilde*

DECISION #3
Self Identity

G rowing up, I had to wade through the intricate web of traditional Chinese family values. My parents' dreams became the guidelines for my life. Their sacrifice to leave China for a better future for me in America with glorious careers of success and prominence is immeasurable. My mother, who was once a respected physician, now bears the burden of her limited knowledge of the English language, yet she humbly worked low wage jobs.

I *had* to succeed!

In the face of their unwavering determination and selflessness, I honored their sacrifice and felt a deep responsibility to pave the way for their success.

The expectations placed on me were high, and the aspirations and unspoken pressures of my family were heavily lurking. I realized that I embody the hopes and dreams of my parents and am responsible for carrying on the resilience and ambition they left behind. The weight of their sacrifice was a constant reminder that I must overcome all obstacles and prove myself worthy of their unwavering belief in my potential.

I got straight A's and excelled in school.

Music band? I'm in.

Orchestra? Sure thing.

Teacher's assistant? Yes, I'm the best.

Whatever it takes.

Every setback I experienced became a catalyst for my determination; every failure was a thrust for my relentless pursuit of success. I realized I could not afford to get lost or suffer self-doubt. Seeing my mother's tireless efforts, as her hands aged from simple work, ignited my heart. I had a constant urge to acquire knowledge, excel academically, and bridge the gap between the past and the future.

But while I struggled to live up to my family's expectations, I also embarked on a personal journey of finding myself. I struggled to balance cultural commitments with my own passions and individual pursuits. It was important to find a harmonious crossroads which allowed me to follow my own path while, at the same time, respecting my roots. I realized my parents' success was not just about professional achievements but about embodying values such as perseverance, honesty, and filial piety.

Through perseverance and relentless determination, I have gradually carved out an identity for myself, exploring my passions and embracing my cultural heritage at the same time. I pursued an education which combined my parents' wishes with my own interests, seeking a balance between my parents' vision for my future and the realization of my own personal dreams. It was not an easy journey but a delicate dance to blend tradition with modernity, gratitude with ambition, and harmony with self-expression.

I am deeply grateful for the sacrifices my parents made in moving me forward in life. After some time, I realized their hopes for me were grounded in my true happiness and fulfillment rather than some predetermined definition of success. Their love pushed the boundaries of conventional expectations, and I learned to embrace their journey as an opportunity to build a life that respects both their sacrifices and my own individuality.

Ultimately, I want to find fulfillment and meaning within myself, not just try to make my parents proud. I recognize success as a complex concept which transcends societal expectations and cultural traditions. It includes personal growth, true happiness, and the pursuit of passions which align with who you really are. By embracing the values instilled in me by my family and integrating them with my own aspirations, I navigate the intricate web of my heritage while weaving the threads of my own unique identity.

During my time in middle school, I enthusiastically delved into the world of acting, attending lessons and even signing up with a casting agency. Each audition was a unique experience as the casting directors welcomed me with obvious enthusiasm, believing that Lucy Liu had enriched their presence. But their elation quickly turned to glaring disappointment when they found out I wasn't the famous actress they were hoping for.

"Oh, she's not THE Lucy Liu" is a phrase that continues to ring in my ears decades later, but I love my name and even decided to keep it after marriage. Still, the limiting belief of my name—Lucy Liu—stuck with me for years.

Being from Los Angeles, I used to even make restaurant reservations in my mom's name to avoid hearing the hostess say, "Are you THE Lucy Liu?"

Someone out there was already exceedingly legendary by that name, so surely I would always be a nobody. I thought to myself, *You certainly don't see another famous Julia Roberts or Angelina Jolie out there, right?* It just doesn't happen. And what's worse is I absolutely adore the woman people refer to as "THE Lucy Liu." She is exceptionally talented as an artist, actress, and director. So, while I can't blame her, I don't want to sabotage myself either.

The struggle is real.

Maybe you have a similar story. Maybe your name is too long, too short, or too difficult to pronounce. Maybe, like I was, you are embarrassed about a part of yourself. Maybe you feel you are less than someone else, or maybe you once felt you were a disappointment to someone. Whatever these thoughts may be, I've learned that they are limiting beliefs.

But what exactly is a "limiting belief"? It is a false belief we acquire as a result of making an incorrect conclusion about something in life—much like I did about my name. It took me nearly a decade of personal development and self-discovery to overcome that particular belief, as well as other fears of mine. But when I finally embraced the discomfort and stared at my fears head-on, I came out of it lighter and less fearful. I let go of thinking too much.

I practiced acceptance, knowing that fighting any emotion would magnify it. Only by practicing acceptance can ease and peace be achieved. Shifting to a mindset of acceptance and abundance allowed me to show up with my attention fully grounded in the present and experience heightened levels of awareness, happiness, and wisdom.

Looking back, those years of disappointment catapulted my personal growth. They forced me to face the challenge of overcoming adversity head-on, teaching me how to regain my shattered confidence and get out of the proverbial sphere—a skill that proved essential in the years to come. I developed resilience along with an inner strength to move on.

Accepting my true identity was a natural consequence of these experiences. Instead of being crushed by the weight of unfulfilled expectations, I decided to see it as a steppingstone on the path to self-discovery. I began to recognize my unique qualities and soon realized it was my personality all along that really set me apart. In a world so often focused on conformity, I learned the extraordinary power of authenticity and self-acceptance.

This valuable life skill I learned at an early age changed me in every aspect of life. It instilled in me the tenacity to face challenges head-on, a belief in my own worth and abilities, and an unwavering determination to accept who I am. I am grateful for the early struggles which ultimately strengthened my spirit and taught me the importance of resilience and unwavering confidence.

Looking back on my journey, I now realize how those auditions were a turning point in my transformation which shaped me into the strong and confident person I am today. They no longer represent moments of disappointment, but rather, they are reminders of my resilience, my ability to exceed the expectations of others, and my unwavering commitment to self-improvement. I am forever grateful for the valuable life lessons I learned during those formative years. This lesson has undoubtedly influenced my path and has given me the strength to face life's challenges with grace, strength, and unwavering faith in my own master. After all, life doesn't get easier; we merely get stronger and more resilient.

JOURNAL PROMPT #3

I made a decision to embrace my identity. *Which part of your identity would you like to embrace more?*

_____

_____

_____

_____

_____

_____

_____

_____

_____

_____

_____

_____

_____

"Those who are free
of resentful thoughts
surely find peace."

—*Buddha*

DECISION #4
Choose Positivity

Self-limiting beliefs are the most probable beliefs to prevent us from reaching our maximum potential. We form limiting ideas to protect ourselves from future pain and uncertainties. They typically emerge during our early years in response to harsh experiences. We form our own, often flawed, assumptions about life based on our experiences. These assumptions become firmly imprinted in our subconscious minds and manifest as limiting beliefs which influence much of what we think, say, and do.

Being a child of immigrant parents had its own limiting self-beliefs and discrimination attached to it. For one, English was my second language. This resulted in the limiting belief that my English wasn't good enough. And I still feel this way sometimes, even though I graduated from UCLA—a top university in the United States. I contemplated and postponed my decision for quite a while to launch a podcast. I had assumptions or perceptions about myself and how others would see me. Some of these assumptions limit me personally.

How do I know this? Because they held me back from achieving what I'm capable of. I eventually decided to stop thinking and just take action to launch my podcast. My first step to overcoming these self-limiting beliefs was identifying them. Launching my podcast led to another stage of uncertainty. Once I made this decision, fear of the unknown snuggled up to me tightly, and I thought things like:

What if people think I'm not qualified to have a podcast?

What if people think I'm riding off the success of THE Lucy Liu's name?

What if people judge me or believe I think I'm better than others?

What if I have zero listeners?

What if I get bad reviews?

The list went on and on forever. Then, I remembered what I'd been preaching on the dozens of guest podcast interviews I'd done: I need to reframe this situation by retraining my mindset. I find that a positive mindset is geared toward motivation. I reminded myself that there is always a way, and I have the power to turn negatives into positives, like these:

What if people relate to my stories?

What if my listeners can't wait to tune in every week to my latest episode?

What if I get messages from listeners about how helpful I was to their lives?

The more I thought about the positive possibilities, the more determined I was to make these my reality. I devised new beliefs to make sense of my aspirations and to give myself a stable foundation for navigating them.

Our journey will always be decked out with pain, risks, laughter, and joy. Honor each season of life; we can't just pick the seasons of our path we want to experience. Life is an all-inclusive ride, and learning to acknowledge the fact that there will always be uncertainty will allow our experiences to be more meaningful and joyful, regardless of what life throws at us.

There is nothing wrong with identifying what I lack. It is beneficial if it encourages me to work toward improvements. However, it can also make me resentful of others who have it or make me feel bad about myself for not having it. All of these feelings gradually become self-limiting. Instead of focusing on the lack of "something," especially the lack of certainty, I stopped comparing myself to others and developed gratitude for the things I enjoy or possess. I started focusing on my abundance, including things like:

I am breathing now.

I own a house.

I own a car.

I have clothes and shoes to wear.

I am beyond grateful for all that I already have, and I'm going to enjoy today.

I made a firm decision to always focus on the positives. I decided to always grow on the abundance. This decision helped me overcome my self-doubts and my personal limiting beliefs to make a triumph.

This ex-overachiever and recovering perfectionist let go of the weight of fear and chose to live a thriving life as an unshakable optimist. As a loving wife, motivated mother, and easygoing entrepreneur, I now make it my mission to help women go from feeling stuck to experiencing full clarity with rock-star confidence. We are the masters of our being; we are in charge of our thoughts, and we are our personality. Knowing who you are and what you stand for in life can help to give you a strong sense of self-confidence. Self-awareness is also linked to confidence. When we know ourselves, it becomes easier to live a life true to our core values. It becomes acceptable to break cultural norms and shatter glass ceilings.

What I wish for you is to do what energizes you for a living and to wake up each day with a smile because another chance for rebirth has been given to you. Embrace life and discover all it has to offer. You should see the world and enjoy the simple pleasures for yourself. If it isn't enough to make you want to see how great life is, then consider the counterintuitive beauty of just living once. Feel alive because the world needs more people who are alive and awake.

Our circumstances in life are neutral—we get to decide if they are positive or negative. We are all natural-born masters of spinning ourselves into negative spirals, but I now pride myself on mastering the skill to pull myself and others out of the overwhelming situations. Life has many ups and downs. You might think you've got it all figured out one day. Then, all of a sudden, you're hit with a curve ball. You are not alone in experiencing these emotions. Everyone must confront their own set of challenges, but learning how to overcome obstacles will help you stay focused.

Say to yourself just as I usually say: I am unique, and I am somebody.

Even if I only help change the life of one listener, I will have made my contribution to creating a better world. I have unshakable faith that I was called on Earth to make those contributions, and I will do so for the rest of my life. This life has some miraculous things to offer, and the world wouldn't be the same without you. Embrace everything life has to offer because your life will not be the same tomorrow or even in an hour. Take in life while you can because it's too good to resist.

JOURNAL PROMPT #4

I made the decision to always focus on the positives. I decided to always focus on the abundance and let abundance grow. *On a scale of 1 to 10, how firm are you on your decision to always choose positivity?*

_____

_____

_____

_____

_____

_____

_____

_____

_____

_____

_____

_____

_____

"The most effective way to do it is to do it."

—*Amelia Earheart*

DECISION #5
Stop Waiting

So many of us spend the majority of our lives waiting for the reassurance that we are ready to go after what we've always wanted—whether it's leaving a toxic relationship, moving to a new place, quitting the job you hate, or starting a new business. We act as if a big neon sign that says "You're ready!" is going to miraculously drop in front of our house.

But we all know that's not how it works. And I hate to break it to you, but if you were waiting for a sign of any sort, then this is it.

If someone had asked me four years ago if I was going to start my own podcast, then my answer would have been an undoubted "no." At the time, I was new to the world of podcasts and had yet to experience the fascination of podcasts attracting millions of listeners around the world. But fate mysteriously pushed me to an unexpected passion. It all started with a surprise invitation to be a podcast guest.

I had no idea what to expect, but my curiosity was intrigued, so I decided to use this opportunity to enter the audio storytelling field. As the host asked questions and conversations unfolded, I was intrigued by the format. I was deeply moved by the ability to communicate ideas, share stories, and have meaningful dialogue through the power of the spoken word.

With each subsequent interview, my fascination with podcasts grew, and I began to see their unique potential for personal expression and connection. The medium explored diverse topics, invited insightful guests, and provided a platform for delving into the depths of the human experience. I realized that podcasts have an amazing ability to break down boundaries, foster a sense of community, and invite listeners to join me on my journey of exploration and discovery. Driven by the passion ignited within me, I decided to take a bold step and create my own podcast. This prospect both excited and intimidated me. It meant breaking new ground and taking on the dual role of host and narrator. But my newfound love for the medium pushed me forward and forced me to turn my vision into a reality.

With careful planning and unwavering determination, I undertook the difficult task of conceptualizing and launching my own podcast in 45 days. I meticulously honed my interviewing skills and my ability to craft thought-provoking questions which would elicit deep insights from my guests. As the podcast's release date approached, I felt a strong mix of anticipation and tension along with the exhilaration of embarking on a creative endeavor which had been unimaginable just a few years ago.

If you had asked me four years ago if I would ever write a book, the answer would also be a definite "no." Even though I had straight A's in English class, I always thought my English wasn't good enough because English wasn't my first language. This book had been in my mind for three years, but it only took one month of action to get it done.

I am no one special, but I am unique as you ALL are. Did I wait for when I was ready? No, I didn't wait. I thought if my podcast or book helps even just one soul, then I will have done my part of contributing to a better world.

I'm just here to remind you that anything is possible, there is always a way, and you get to decide to the kind of life you live. I don't care about what others might think of me, and I don't look at what others are doing. No, I just do my thing! And I do it without losing myself or sacrificing my priorities.

When I first wanted to start a podcast, I told myself I was going to ask a stranger on Instagram to be my first guest, and if she says yes, then I'll take it as a sign to launch my podcast in September. So, I did exactly that. I befriended Jennifer Sutto through a shoutout from another coach friend. Two months later, I hosted my first podcast episode with my first guests Jennifer and her sister Steph Sutto. Did I believe at the time she would say yes? Absolutely! I read her Instagram posts and watched all her stories, so I knew she was super friendly in the online space. And I took landing on her profile to be my sign. But the thing is, I didn't need a sign. I create my own signs, and I give myself permission to take anything I want as a sign.

One of my past clients messaged me after she heard me talk on a podcast, and she thought my podcast was her sign to become a life coach. After working together only briefly, she already has the most amazing website, has her program ready, and is ready to impact the world. She didn't wait any longer for a sign; she was openly ready to receive whatever was given to her as a sign, and she took action.

In this unexpected journey, I discovered my voice and the power of storytelling to create change and foster connection. The podcasting landscape has become my canvas—where I tell stories, highlight important issues, and invite listeners into a world of shared experiences and collective growth.

Looking back, it's amazing how my initial indifference to podcasts turned into an unwavering passion which has shaped such an important part of my life. Going from interviewee to podcast host was a transformative experience for me. It allowed me to embrace the unexpected, nurture my creativity, and unlock the incredible potential within me.

Today, I have proven that passion can emerge in unexpected places and that when you open yourself up to new experiences, you can uncover hidden talents and embark on an amazing journey of self-discovery.

The moment you decide to wait, you start calculating a list of reasons as to why right now isn't the right time. Then, you double think and triple think in your head as to why something you want won't or can't work out. You will then absolutely be convinced that the timing isn't right. If this continues for the rest of your life, then you will never have what you truly want in life. And by that, I don't mean just materialistic things but also intangible things like happiness and freedom.

Yes, you can meditate.

Yes, you can quit whatever you want to quit.

Yes, you can wake up earlier.

Yes, you have the time.

Yes, you can do it.

Stop giving yourself excuses. Take whatever life throws at you and make your next move. Whether you're taking massive leaps or baby steps, even turtle speed forward is still moving forward. But trust me on these two things:

If you think you need help, ask for it.

If you want change in any way, start today.

JOURNAL PROMPT #5

I made a decision to create signs and just go for it rather than waiting for a sign. *What are you waiting to make happen now? Take reading this book as your sign!*

_____

_____

_____

_____

_____

_____

_____

_____

_____

_____

_____

_____

_____

"Gratitude can transform common days into Thanksgiving, turn routine jobs into joy, and change ordinary opportunities into blessings."

— *William Arthur Ward*

DECISION #6

Gratitude

As we journey through life, our perspectives often undergo profound transformations, leading us to reevaluate our values and priorities. Childhood, with its innocence and boundless imagination, is typically the time when you see the world through rose-tinted glasses and feel like the richest and happiest being on the planet. For many, this feeling fades over time and is replaced by a more complex and nuanced understanding of wealth and happiness.

This was the case for me. In elementary school, I was the sum of contentment and felt I had all the best things in the world. Material possessions like a piece of candy, friendships like someone I didn't even know walking home with me, and just life's simplest pleasures seemed to melt into a tapestry of pure joy. I looked forward to each holiday and to each rising sun, and nothing could have stopped me from enjoying every passing second to the fullest.

As we transition from a carefree childhood to a complex adulthood, the simple joys that once filled our hearts with endless happiness fade away, and we start to seek meaning and fulfillment. This transformation is a common rite of passage and, unfortunately, often coincides with the advent of materialistic pursuits, where the acquisition of more possessions leads to lost abundance and happiness. It leads us to falsely believe we can restore that shine we once had as a child.

And of course, I also fell into this trap. As I began my journey into adulthood, I started to experience the gradual dwindle of the satisfaction I once cherished. The pressures and the responsibilities of life can overshadow the childlike wonder which once defined our world. In the midst of this change, I was trying to regain the wealth and wellbeing I once had, and society's dominant image of materialism seemed to be the answer. Money began to fly into my life as I pursued my goals and ambitions. Attracted by the promise that having more possessions would lead to a better life, I accepted it as my plan to restore the happiness I thought I had lost.

But this pursuit of material possessions soon revealed its downside. The more you have, the less excitement and happiness you feel when you first get something new, leaving you with a feeling of emptiness and dissatisfaction. The fulfillment I sought will always be unattainable. It was as if I were chasing a shadow that seemed to be on the horizon, promising satisfaction but never delivering. The result was a never-ending cycle of wanting more, leaving me still constantly dissatisfied and longing for the next shiny object to fill the void.

I learned too late that the pursuit of materialism blinds us to the essence of abundance and happiness. True satisfaction does not come from external possessions and achievements alone. It is an inner state which emerges from gratitude, mindfulness, and a deeper connection with yourself and others. I'm glad, even in the midst of this struggle, I always had a glimmer of hope. My experience offers valuable lessons about the power of self-reflection and self-awareness.

The turning point in life came when I began to understand the power of gratitude. Gratitude is the art of recognizing and appreciating the wealth which already exists in our lives, such as loving relationships, health, personal growth, and the beauty of the world around us. It is a powerful perspective shift which changes our perception of reality.

This shift in perspective is a natural part of the human experience. As we age, we become more sensitive to life's complexities and challenges. This pursuit of material possessions, which once brought instant gratification, begins to feel empty and unfulfilling. We realize true wealth and happiness lies beyond material possessions and fleeting pleasures.

Being grateful for what you already have creates satisfaction and fulfillment, turning even the simplest moments into sources of joy. Gratitude doesn't mean ignoring life's challenges or pretending everything is perfect. Rather, we face challenges with resilience and a positive attitude, knowing there is always something to be grateful for, even in difficult situations.

I experienced a profound shift in my understanding of true wealth when I started to embrace a mindset of gratitude. It became clear to me that prosperity includes not only material prosperity but also spiritual prosperity. Possessing material wealth can bring temporary happiness, but it cannot replace the lasting fulfillment gratitude brings.

I also realized that happiness is not a product of chance or external circumstances. Rather, happiness is associated with being grateful for the blessings of life—both large and small. Embracing gratitude fosters a sense of connection with the world and an appreciation for the bundles of possibilities surrounding us every day.

My journey taught me that true wealth and happiness is an inner state of being, based on an attitude of gratitude, an appreciation of life's gifts, and a willingness to share those blessings with others. It is a journey of self-discovery and understanding, revealing the limitless potential of each individual. In a world obsessed with getting and comparing, my story is a reminder that simple acts of gratitude can change our lives. Gratitude can bring us back to the joy and satisfaction we once felt as children, even though we are now more aware of the world and our place in it.

As you continue to cultivate gratitude, your life becomes an ever-evolving tapestry of joy, wealth, and happiness. It will be measured not by material possessions but by the abundance of love, kindness, and gratitude in your heart.

Ultimately, the pursuit of true happiness may lead you on a journey of self-discovery where you embrace your unique passions and values and align your actions with those that bring you true joy. This path may not always be easy, but it can lead you to a more authentic and meaningful life where the true essence of abundance and happiness illuminates your soul.

JOURNAL PROMPT #6

I made a decision to live life daily with gratitude. *What are you grateful for today?*

_____

_____

_____

_____

_____

_____

_____

_____

_____

_____

_____

_____

_____

"Nature does not
hurry, yet everything is
accomplished."

—*Lao Tzu*

DECISION #7
Slow Down

Slow down to accomplish more! Yup, it sounds backwards, but slowing down is actually the best way to accomplish faster.

Go faster.

Do more.

Hustle. Hustle.

Chase the next level. Chase the next shiny object.

Many workplaces encourage a "hustle" mentality and reward those who work long hours to achieve quick, tangible results. This culture can put pressure on us to continue striving for excellence, even at the cost of our own wellbeing. Many quit traditional jobs to seek freedom, only to find themselves working even more hours in their own business.

Economic uncertainty, rising costs of living, and the need to ensure financial security all lead us to continually strive for greater success and financial security. Even worse, the new digital age has created a culture of immediate gratification where we expect immediate results and immediate rewards. This mindset can lead to impatience and a constant desire for the next achievement or milestone.

These societal and environmental factors teach us to work harder to achieve the "all American dream." I've been there myself. I worked way too hard in my twenties. I remember those days vividly where I would work until midnight or even until dawn the next day. Society often expects us to reach certain milestones by a certain age or follow a predetermined path to success. Because of this, people often feel the pressure to keep striving for the next level of achievement and to do so at any cost.

The pursuit of progress and personal growth is essential to development and fulfillment, but the constant search for the next shiny object can have negative consequences. It can lead to burnout and stress, which is where I found myself. At 24 years old, I found myself short of breath. I frequently gasped for air and took deep breaths which would create so much pressure in my lungs, yet I still felt short of breath. Chronic yawning was also unstoppable. It worsened quickly when chest pains were added to the mix. I was certain my heart was soon going to fail on me! Many checkups and doctor visits later, I was diagnosed with burnout and stress.

WHAT?!

How can burnout and stress alone cause so much physical change in the body? I was astonished to face this reality. I had to combat this toxic hustle culture. I had to cultivate mindfulness. I needed to set more realistic goals and find satisfaction in my current situation.

I also started to worry. I was afraid that in all my busyness, I would miss out on all the most beautiful parts of life. While many personal coaches and social media influencers flash their private jets, fancy cars, and hustle lifestyle, truly successful leaders and entrepreneurs who are actually happy and creating lasting results in their lives know that slowing down builds the true foundation for their success. It took me a decade to learn the importance of slowing down to accomplish more. I want you to realize this earlier in life than I did. I want you to emphasize the value of meaningful experiences, deep connections, and personal wellbeing over material possessions and society's standard of what success looks like. I want to help you shift your focus from constant pursuit to a more balanced and fulfilling way of life.

Now, I schedule time to do nothing on purpose. I go on frequent vacations with my family and feel absolutely no guilt for not working while I'm on vacation. I encourage you to unapologetically incorporate periods of stillness to help you ensure enhanced productivity and wellbeing.

When slowing down, focus on what's truly important in life. When we live busy and distracted lives, we lose sight of the people and things that matter most to us. Slow down and re-evaluate your values and priorities every six months or so. Re-evaluate if your current routine is helping you stay healthy—both mentally and physically.

Psychologists and doctors are talking about this new condition called "hurry sickness." It is a form of modern day anxiety fueled by our constant state of busyness and trying to squeeze in just one more thing into your already packed schedule. And this starts first thing in the morning. Do you rush to get up when the alarm rings? Or do you get up slowly from bed? Instead of rolling straight out of bed and into your life, set your alarm clock earlier and take time to welcome the day. Spend a few minutes to gently stretch in bed, listen to a motivational speech to start your morning, or make your bed. Remove any rush and set the tone for the rest of your day.

When you drive and get on the road, intentionally slow down and actually drive the speed limit. Is it hard? If it feels difficult, if you want to beat traffic, if you are thinking about how to beat Google Maps by a couple minutes, then it's time to force yourself to slow down. When you physically force yourself to slow down, you can begin training your mind to mentally slow down. And when you have peace of mind, you'll start to see sceneries and opportunities you might otherwise miss. If you want to go a little further, take some time and spend it in silence. In our noisy world, silence is something we must intentionally choose. I've gone on silent retreats in the past where we don't talk for a weekend, and let me tell you—that experience is still very eye-opening when I think about it to this day.

When you slow down, you are able to make good decisions—better decisions than if your mind was more occupied. When you slow down and engage in slower-paced activities like meditation, brain fog clears away, and you see clarity. And clarity is priceless. Once you stop rushing through life, you will be amazed at how much more life you have time for. You will be amazed at how much more productive you become because you now value your time, leaving precious moments for your true values and priorities.

Slow down and be your best. Life is not a race. It's a playground to radiate your uniqueness and shine your light. So, have fun on your journey to slowing down yet accomplishing more.

JOURNAL PROMPT #7

I made a decision to slow down in life to achieve more. *Instead of writing your next to-do list, write an un-do list and list all the things you need to stop doing in life.*

_____

_____

_____

_____

_____

_____

_____

_____

_____

_____

_____

_____

_____

_____

"Uncertainty is the only certainty there is, and knowing how to live with insecurity is the only security."

—*John Allen Paulos*

DECISION #8

Uncertainty

As human beings, our intellect always longs for clarity and certainty; however, the reality is we often find ourselves in uncertainty. Whether these uncertainties are caused by external circumstances like the pandemic we just experienced or inner thoughts, uncertain time periods in our lives are inevitable. I've learned through the past decade to have patience with everything that remains unsolved in my heart.

If I've learned anything from Covid-19, it would be the famous quote by mathematician and professor John Allen Paulos: "Uncertainty is the only certainty there is, and knowing how to live with insecurity is the only security you truly have." The biggest mindset shift is going from feeling like you are doomed for not knowing what's ahead to recognizing that the possibilities are endless. Possibilities are what make uncertainty truly fascinating.

Let me share a personal story with you. In the early years of our marriage, the different approaches to travel between my husband and I always created tension and anxiety. His short-lived and spontaneous personality clashed with my desire for planned schedules, frequently causing arguments and feelings of insecurity. He never had any trips planned ahead of time. I was nervous at first because I hadn't planned the trip in advance. The unknown made it difficult to plan and manage other aspects of life. The lack of a clear roadmap led to confusion and anxiety, and it seemed I would fall into a state of dread as I dealt with the unpredictability of each journey we took together.

But as time went by, I realized that trying to change him was impossible, and it was much easier to change myself. I chose to change my own perspective and mindset. That change has allowed me to embrace the beauty of spontaneity and find joy in the unexpected. I made the conscious decision to take my focus away from the uncertainty which was plaguing me and instead enjoy the spontaneous excitement that last-minute travel can bring. Letting go of the need for rigid planning allowed me to open my mind to the beauty of surprise and the thrill of spontaneous adventure. Each journey becomes a delightful mystery, evoking surprise and anticipation like never before.

With this new attitude, I began to recognize the beauty of life being in the present moment. The lack of stringent plans allowed us to free ourselves from the constraints of pre-scheduling and fully immerse ourselves in the present experience. It was like a breath of fresh air, freeing me from the burden of overthinking and empowering me to enjoy every spontaneous moment. The thrill of not knowing the destination or activity in advance becomes an adventure in itself, kindling the wonder and curiosity of a child which has since been forgotten as an adult.

I began to appreciate the spontaneous enjoyment of travel, and I realized the benefits it brought to my relationship with my husband. The shared excitement of embarking on these impromptu journeys together created a deep bond between us and led to memories that will forever be etched in their hearts.

Now, when my husband books a plane ticket for the next morning, I become excited to pack my luggage with my little one, so we can head to the airport and enjoy our spontaneous weekend getaway. You see, none of the outside circumstances changed, but because I changed my mindset, my experience became completely different. This is exactly why I love to preach the importance of mindset because circumstances are always neutral, but you get to decide if it is positive or negative, and when you choose positivity, your reaction will determine your complete experience. Therefore, your mindset will determine your life.

This shift in thinking also affected me in other areas of life. I have become more adaptable, flexible, and willing to accept life's twists and turns. The uncertainty that once caused fear is now an opportunity for growth and discovery, enabling me to face any of life's surprises with new confidence and resilience.

The spontaneity of travel has become a metaphor for embracing the uncertainty life brings. It taught me how letting go of the need for rigid control and embracing spontaneity can lead to unexpected joy and deep personal growth.

I used to also hate aging because the inevitable passage of time that comes with aging is scary to think about. When we are young, we often try to avoid growing old out of fear of the uncertainties and unknowns that lie ahead. We may be filled with uncertainty about the future, the path ahead, the challenges we face, and the changes that await us. Fear of the unknown can be overwhelming, so we resist the idea of getting older.

However, as life progresses, we witness the beauty and grace of aging with renewed joy and gratitude. The accumulation of life lessons gradually gives us the gift of life.

Wisdom.

And uncertainty is the best kind of wisdom!

Wisdom is the precious jewel of knowledge and insight we have in our hearts and minds. It is the ability to see through the essence of a situation, see things beyond the surface, and face life with a deeper understanding of its complexities. Wisdom comes from a combination of experience, reflection, and a willingness to embrace uncertainty as a source of learning and growth.

As we age, we realize uncertainty is not a force to be feared but a source of wisdom. Embracing the unknown opens the door to new possibilities, opportunities, and discoveries. Life is unpredictable, but you can embrace change with grace and adaptability, knowing it will be a wonderful journey.

Wisdom teaches us that life is not about controlling every aspect or having every answer. Rather, it is important to embrace anxiety with an open mind. It encourages us to approach the unknown with a sense of adventure and see it as an invitation to learn, evolve, and discover the hidden treasures that lie within.

Through the wisdom of aging, we learn to let go of our desire for absolute security and perfection. We understand that the imperfections and uncertainties of life make it beautiful and full of surprises. Embracing uncertainty promotes resilience and flexibility, allowing you to calmly weather life's storms with grace.

While we embrace the wisdom of uncertainties, we also value the interconnectedness of all life experiences. Moments of joy, sorrow, love, and loss melt into a deep tapestry of understanding. We recognize every step we take, every decision we make, and every moment we experience as a contribution to our growth and wisdom.

By embracing uncertainty as our best piece of wisdom, we free ourselves from the burden of our youth's fears and anxieties. As we get older, we learn to appreciate the present and embrace the beautiful uncertainty that lies ahead.

How you react to uncertainty will determine the transformation of your life and soul. Use the times of uncertainty as a compass to guide you to new growth ahead. Simplicity, faith, and a positive mindset are the keys to thriving in your life. Keep things simple, don't overthink, don't overreact, have faith and always believe there is a way because everything is happening for the best. Remember to intentionally choose to be positive.

The ability to embrace your uncertainties is the only way to your freedom. Enjoy the beauty of becoming. When nothing is certain, anything is possible.

JOURNAL PROMPT #8

I made a decision to embrace uncertainty. *Are you with me?*

_____

_____

_____

_____

_____

_____

_____

_____

_____

_____

_____

_____

_____

"**Calmness is the cradle of power.**"

—*Josiah Gilbert Holland*

DECISION #9

Emotional Hijack

H ave you ever cried yourself to sleep?

I have. Countless times—so many times I can't just tell one story here.

Even when the details of the situation start to fade away in memory, the feelings of heartache, disappointment, worthlessness, and frustration leave lasting imprints in our hearts.

Crying to sleep is a highly emotional experience which can result from a variety of difficult and stressful situations. You've probably experienced it too in one way or another. Maybe it was the loss of a loved one, a heartbreak, or even loneliness and isolation. Even simple daily chores can add up, causing you to feel overwhelmed with life responsibilities, powerless to change your circumstances, or a loss of control. Then, we can also experience betrayal, rejection, emotional abuse, or even traumatic experiences such as car accidents or natural disasters. Some may face chronic diseases or watching a loved one suffer. During the pandemic, many experienced feelings of loss and struggled with the uncertainty of the future, which can trigger feelings of sadness and tears in moments of vulnerability.

I say this a lot: all of our emotions are valid. Why? Because our emotions are rooted in our subconscious mind; as long as we are a living, breathing being, we're going to have emotions.

But in a worst case scenario, we get emotionally hijacked. An emotional hijack refers to a personal emotional response that is immediate, overwhelming, and out of measure with the actual stimulus because it has been triggered from a much more significant emotional threat. This term was first coined by psychologist Daniel Goleman in 1995. Another way to explain this is emotional hijack is a situation in which the part of your brain that serves as your emotional processor hijacks or even bypasses your normal reasoning process.

An example of emotional hijack can be when you suddenly snap at someone after they have only said one word. It isn't really the word that triggered the anger; it's the emotions behind what happened previously. You might regret your own reactions and hate yourself for being a slave to your own emotions. You become programmed to react in a certain way to a specific set of circumstances, leaving you with a lack of self-control. If you have ever felt this way, then you were being hijacked by your emotions.

A lot of people use emotions and feelings interchangeably, but I don't think that's very accurate. Feelings are the reactions to circumstances, and they can come after the emotion. For example, we sometimes would say "I'm feeling very stressed out" after something happened. But the feeling can be different for everyone because of the different thoughts we process. Someone else might feel excited after the exact same situation. So you see, we get to determine our thoughts after the situation and that in turn determines our feelings towards the situation.

The good news is you can control your thoughts or practice changing negative thoughts into positive ones. This is the best way to stop emotional hijacking. The better news is that even if you can't control your thoughts to always be positive, you can create a positive thought immediately after a negative one. Other ways to stop emotional hijacking include changing scenery or focusing on taking longer, deeper breaths before reacting. You can literally get up and walk elsewhere. If you are having a conversation, you can end the conversation or even come back to it rather than allowing impulsive reactions to cloud your judgment, having a negative impact on your words and behaviors.

My life was profoundly transformed after I learned the word "equanimity." It is my absolute favorite word in the English dictionary. According to the Merriam-Webster dictionary, equanimity is the evenness of mind, especially under stress. Oxford defines it as calmness and composure, especially in a difficult situation. Here is an example sentence: "She accepted both the good and the bad with equanimity." How powerful is that? To cultivate a habit of mind which is only rarely disturbed under great strain.

Before I lived with equanimity, I rode on many emotional roller coaster rides. You know, this is where we experience intense elation during positive events and a deep depression during difficult times. In layman's terms, I had a lot of mood swings. Without equanimity, I could easily become agitated, impatient, or overwhelmed by everyday stressors. I binge watched sobby dramas to avoid discomfort and pain. My mind was full of excessive rumination and worry, constantly swinging between the dreaded past and the doomed future, robbing me of my joy in the present moment. And there were definitely marriage issues as a result. The lack of equanimity meant we both would react impulsively or take things personally, which led to conflicts and misunderstandings.

After learning to live with equanimity, I started to have emotional stability and experience a sense of inner stillness and balance amid life's ups and downs. I learned to be less responsive to external situations and instead respond to situations with a sense of detachment and mindfulness rather than being driven by impulsive reactions. Calmness helped me accept the imperfections of life and recognize that both pleasant and unpleasant experiences are impermanent. I began to experience freedom of attachment and gained a deeper understanding of life's simple pleasures. Living with equanimity reduces stress and anxiety by allowing us to face challenges with greater receptivity and peace of mind. Calmness promoted better communication, empathy, and understanding in my marriage, and I became more resilient in the face of adversity and able to bounce back from setbacks with strength and adaptability. And the best part of all, I became the queen of decision making. I've moved away from impulsive emotions and consider the big picture to make decisions easily with clarity and wisdom.

Always remember that our goal is to maintain a composed state of awareness and to be mindful and conscious of our reactions. Choose your thoughts intentionally. Believe that you are in control. Even when you're being emotionally hijacked, you will have the absolute power to stop it right there. You are the CEO of this organization called YOUR life!

JOURNAL PROMPT #9

I made a decision to always stop my emotions from hijacking my life and to live a life with equanimity. *From a scale of 1 to 10, with 10 being fully living with equanimity, where are you at now? What areas can you improve?*

_____

_____

_____

_____

_____

_____

_____

_____

_____

_____

_____

_____

_____

_____

_____

"The difference
between an optimist
and a pessimist is
that the optimist sees
the donut, and the
pessimist sees the hole."

— *Oscar Wilde*

DECISION #10

Optimism

Regardless of what challenges you face in life, I believe being optimistic and having confidence in yourself is the first step towards success. Once you believe you can do something, you're already halfway there!

Optimism simply makes life more enjoyable and meaningful. Perpetual optimism then is the force multiplier. As a proud eternal optimist myself, I can barely put into words the magnitude of power optimism has in our lives.

But it wasn't always that way.

As you've already read in previous chapters, my many limiting beliefs in life hindered me from living with optimism at a younger age. That lack of optimism fueled self-doubt, making it difficult to believe in my own abilities and potential to accomplish something great in this lifetime. I was ready to be the average Jane I thought I was born to be. I wasn't looking for any solutions to my loss of motivation, and my pessimistic mindset made it difficult to see potential solutions to my problems or opportunities in difficult situations, leaving me often feeling stuck in my situations. I mean, life wasn't bad. I had more than I needed, but a negative attitude definitely led to a lack of enthusiasm, emotional withdrawal, and a tendency to focus on my past failures. My mind was always preoccupied with worries about possible negative effects, and even moving forward in life on autopilot brought anxiety and stress.

Through two decades of personal development and investing in myself, I've learned finally that optimism empowers us to face challenges with hope and a positive attitude, allowing us to find joy in our journey despite uncertainty. Optimism increases emotional resilience, improves relationships, and promotes wellbeing, thus contributing the most to my fulfilling and satisfying life.

After cultivating optimism, I now have a positive outlook on life, expect positive outcomes, and see the potential for good things to happen in a variety of situations. And even when the outcome may not be as positive as expected, optimism makes it easier to face challenges, adapt to change, and bounce back from setbacks with a hopeful attitude. When approached with challenges, I maintain a proactive attitude and always believe there is a solution.

Thirty-year-old Lucy was ready to hit the graveyard. But forty-year-old Lucy has the hopeful attitude to pursue all her new life goals and aspirations, and she believes in her ability to achieve them. And best of all, optimism led to my appreciation for the good things and opportunities in each new day, leading to greater happiness and satisfaction in life. It is so fun to build up your confidence muscle and believe in your own growth potential.

If you constantly think optimistically about the future, then you are always thinking about good things that can happen. This flood of positive thoughts can add joy to your life now. And, by having faith and working towards goals to make these good things happen, you are more likely to be proactive when dealing with life's difficulties and stress. Find joy in everything you choose to do, and you will live a joyful life. I'm all about joy and growing in our personal life and business while also having fun—that's why my mastermind group is called the Joyful CEO Mastermind.

Yes, stress is an inevitable part of life, but the way you react and handle it matters the most and determines your entire experience. Optimistic people do not overthink or allow the stress sink in; therefore, there is no place for stress to stay, resulting in only room being left for positivity and happiness.

Optimism enhances your health. So many studies have shown that optimists are more likely to maintain better physical health. Because optimists tend to have lower levels of stress and pain, they usually have stronger immune systems and, therefore, remain healthier and even live longer. Healthy people who are optimistic report they simply feel better.

Optimism enhances your relationships too. Now, let's be real—who wants to talk to a bitter face all the time? No one. So when you radiate sunshine, your life will be filled with more sunshine. A healthy dose of optimism in your relationship or friendship allows you to notice the good things about your partner/friend and see the positive side of situations and a positive outcome for the future.

When I first discovered the quote by Oscar Wilde that says, "The difference between an optimist and a pessimist is that the optimist sees the donut, and the pessimist sees the hole," I literally laughed out loud because there's such a huge difference in these two viewpoints. Which point of view you take can have an enormous impact on your work, health, and life. Who would you rather work with or hang out with, someone who lightens up the day and supports you, or someone who habitually complains about everything and blames others?

Optimism uplevels your productivity as well. High performers are more flexible, resilient, and joyful; they are not stuck in any self-absorbed defensive or negative behaviors. Therefore, they produce higher results in their work.

Optimism is your seed to growing opportunities. Increasing the positive in your day doesn't happen on its own. Opportunities don't appear to be opportunities if you're not positive. You have to consciously deflect the negative, let things go, and have a positive mindset to move forward. We may not be in charge of much in this uncertain world, but we can absolutely control our minds and how we think about what happens to us. And that controls everything. Remember the choice is always yours: is the cup half-full or half-empty? The secret lies in reframing the situation. You will quickly see that the power of optimism will lead you to beautiful new opportunities.

Optimism is a hopeful, positive outlook on the future, on yourself, and on the world around you. Optimism helps you see, feel, and think positively. And remember, you don't have to be born an optimist to use the power of optimism. Optimism is a strength we all possess, so choose to turn the switch on for this magical function to start operating in your life.

JOURNAL PROMPT #10

I made a decision to be an unshakable optimist. *What opportunities are you looking to unlock right now if you choose to be more optimistic?*

_____

_____

_____

_____

_____

_____

_____

_____

_____

_____

_____

_____

_____

_____

"You are exactly where you need to be."

—Unknown

@mslucyliu #confidentandepic

DECISION #11

Embrace

It was a beautiful Sunday evening. I had just put my daughter to bed at eight o'clock that night. This was my usual daily time to listen to podcasts while waiting for her to fall asleep in the dark. I was listening to a podcast episode where the amazing guest of the show, a successful female entrepreneur out of New York, was telling her story about growing up in the city of Rosemead, California—a city where I also once lived. Now to give you some context, Rosemead is a city about 20 minutes east of downtown Los Angeles—a city in which many consider to be less than ideal to live or raise their kids.

In her talk, she expressed a deep desire to distance herself from the city of Rosemead. The reason being she was driven by a yearning for more things beyond the limits of her immediate surroundings. This desire to be free of the limitations and prejudices associated with her homeland is reflected in a longing for growth, opportunity, and new horizons. I think her experiences reflected a common theme found in many personal stories—a discontentment in the current job, location, or state of mind. A desire to escape, go beyond the familiar, and embrace the unknown. This longing for escape can be triggered by a variety of factors, such as seeking new experiences, pursuing dreams and ambitions, or simply discovering a different way of life.

It is important to recognize that each person's view of their homeland is shaped by their circumstances, aspirations, and personal history. Some may think that a town like Rosemead lacks certain aspects, but it's important to recognize that each location has its own strengths, challenges, and untapped potential. Whether or not a current job, location, or state of mind is "ideal" or "not ideal" is completely subjective and varies from person to person.

For this successful entrepreneur, her desire to leave Rosemead became a catalyst for personal growth and an opportunity to challenge herself beyond the immediate environment. It represented the urge for self-discovery and the pursuit of a future which matched her dreams and aspirations.

However, it's worth noting that your relationship with your hometown can change over time. The experiences and lessons of living elsewhere often provide valuable insight and a deeper awareness of one's roots. Many eventually reconnect with their homes, bringing with them new wisdom, new experiences, and a renewed appreciation for where they came from. After all, finding something beyond home can lead to personal growth and fulfillment. But keep in mind, it's not just where we come from that defines us; it's the choices we make, the paths we take, and the resilience we show along the way. Any place, anywhere, regardless of reputation, can be the starting point for an incredible journey of self-discovery and fulfilling dreams.

This particular podcast episode really resonated with me and actually made me almost laugh out loud because I was once in the exact same situation. My parents didn't buy our first house until I was in middle school. Before then, we moved from city to city, the aim being to find a better area with better schools for me. Finally, in the middle of eighth grade, we bought our first condo in our dream city. I was doing great, had straight A's, but I still felt it wasn't enough. I was chasing all the shiny objects in life, I felt behind, and I was never truly happy.

After my sophomore year in high school, I dropped out of high school, despite having straight A's. I wanted to progress in life faster. I was chasing the invisible and impossible. I also longed to escape my past and was seeking new experiences, pursuing dreams and ambitions, and trying to reach a different way of life.

Ultimately, I disciplined myself through a local community college and transferred to UCLA. Once at UCLA, voila, I found out one of my roommates was from the city of Rosemead. Coincidence? Or serendipity? Maybe life was trying to teach me a lesson: I never needed to escape from anything or anywhere. I was never behind. Good enough is a decision, and I learned to embrace every season in life.

Where you are now may just be the best place for you to be and exactly where you should be. What you are doing in life might just be the best thing for you to be doing. When your business explodes it might not match your expectations, but everything is falling into place as it unfolds. All you need to do is enjoy what you have in the present. Every moment holds the potential for growth and happiness, regardless of challenges or perceived shortcomings. Embracing the present allows us to fully experience and recognize the beauty of our current situation.

Life is a wonderful journey full of twists and turns, triumphs and setbacks, and ever-present opportunities for growth and transformation. Sometimes, we wish for a different situation or compare our progress to the expectations set by ourselves or others. But amid this desire for change and comparison, it's important to remember some basic truths.

Nobody can go back in time and start a new beginning, but anyone can start today to create a new ending. Enjoy the journey itself instead of just focusing on the missing pieces or the bottom line. It doesn't matter where you start; it matters where you finish and how you enjoyed the journey along the way! Or better yet, it doesn't matter where you start, as long as you start.

The past cannot be rewritten, but the present has infinite possibilities. Every day is an opportunity to create a new ending. Where your journey starts is important, but what really matters is the journey and where it ends. Every step, no matter how small, will propel you to growth and transformation. No matter where you start, the courage to take the first step drives the wheels of progress.

Maybe you are just starting on your personal development journey or you're on a new entrepreneurial journey. Maybe you are starting to pivot after Covid-19. Anything you are starting will feel new and scary, but I honor your courage and congratulate you on opening your new chapter in life.

JOURNAL PROMPT #11

I made a decision to switch my mentality from escape to embrace. *Which part of your life would you like to embrace?*

_____

_____

_____

_____

_____

_____

_____

_____

_____

_____

_____

_____

"Do something today that your future self will thank you for."

—*Sean Patrick Flanery*

DECISION #12

Thank You

You might have heard this quote before: "Do something today that your future self will thank you for."

But what does that really mean?

It means every single decision you make today will affect your future. That is exactly why I am over the moon passionate about writing this book, to share the decisions I made which positively shaped my life. Invest in yourself today and make conscious decisions to learn and improve yourself so that down the road, when you look back on life, you will thank yourself for the decisions you made today.

When I hear this phrase, it reminds me of my high school job because I absolutely loved my job then. Even after all these years, I'm still happy I made the choice to work part-time at the local bookstore instead of at a clothing store like most of my classmates at school. I am forever grateful for this choice.

To many people, my job was merely a cashier position, but to me, it was my introduction to a whole new world. Through constant restocking and alphabetizing of books, I learned a little bit about every topic, opening up my worldly views. Regardless of my ultimate career path, I know this cashier experience provided valuable skills and advantages.

By working as a cashier, I was offered many opportunities to develop excellent customer service skills. I learned the basics of how to interact with customers, handle requests, resolve issues, and ensure a positive experience. These skills can be applied across a variety of professions and industries where customer interactions are critical.

As a cashier, you can improve your communication and interpersonal skills by interacting with different customers on a daily basis. I learned excellent telephone skills, being sure to listen carefully, articulate information, and adapt my communication style to meet the needs of different customers. These skills are highly valued in any workplace and are essential for building effective professional relationships.

Cashiers often work in fast-paced environments and need to manage their time effectively by multitasking. This allowed me to develop strong organizational skills and the abilities to prioritize tasks and work effectively under pressure. A cashier will never forget the busy scenes from Christmas shopping or the crazy Black Friday sales. These skills are useful in a variety of roles where time management and efficiency are essential.

As a cashier, accuracy is of the utmost importance as you have to process financial transactions and make sure the amount is correct. This encourages a meticulous attention to detail which is a valuable skill in various professions such as accounting, data analysis, and quality control.

As a cashier, you may encounter various challenges and difficult situations like responding to customer complaints, resolving price discrepancies, or resolving technical issues with the checkout system. These experiences will sharpen your problem-solving skills and enable you to think critically and find practical solutions—an asset in any professional environment.

Customer service jobs can be tough at times, especially in the face of demanding customers and challenging situations. But this experience helps you develop resilience, perseverance, and the ability to remain calm under pressure, traits that contribute to personal and professional growth.

Cashiers also often work as part of a team, requiring effective coordination and collaboration. Through this experience, I also developed skills in teamwork, collaboration, and the ability to contribute to a common goal—again, all qualities which are highly desired by employers in any industry or field.

Oh, and I can think of tons of other perks to working at a bookstore like substantial employee discounts on all books and magazines, free uncorrected versions of upcoming books to read, and working in an enjoyable environment—the smell of fresh books and patient co-workers who are also passionate about books still makes me so happy to think about. If you start looking in the right places, there are perks in everything.

While my cashier experience is unique to me and my journey, your past may be different. If you have ever been in a situation where you were not in a position related to your ultimate career goal, just remember that the skills and qualities developed in that role can positively contribute to your future progress. It can provide a solid foundation for all your future endeavors.

We all know our future depends on what we do in our present. So, if you don't shape your present now, you cannot witness the desired result in your future. What kinds of results do you want in your future life? What seeds are you planting? Ask yourself:

Are you investing in yourself?

Are you making decisions embodying the mind of who you want to be?

Are you living life, or are you designing your life?

Is your life in alignment with what you truly want and value?

Who are you taking with you on your journey to your best life?

Now that I have a podcast, I am incredibly thankful for my younger elementary school self to have signed up for speaking classes in order to be a kid storyteller at our local radio station.

Now that I am an unshakable optimist, I am so thankful for each and every negative circumstance that was thrown into my life to teach me a lesson and allow me to practice my resilience.

Now that I coach amazing women on growing their business, I am so thankful for the naive young me for the failed businesses because I know what doesn't work and what not to do.

Now that I coach remarkable females on growing their life, I am so thankful for all the wrong turns I took in life.

Now that I have a coaching business, I am beyond thankful to younger myself for investing in my coaches.

Now that I'm pounding on my keyboard trying to put this book out into the world, I am incredibly grateful I chose to work in that bookstore. Reading became my lifetime hobby, and I am in love with how words have the power to change lives.

Acting with intention today allows your future self to reap the benefits of your present actions. Remember, even small steps, no matter how insignificant they seem now, can lead to major progress and long-term results. So, seize the opportunity to make a difference, fulfill your aspirations, and create a future that your future self will appreciate.

JOURNAL PROMPT #12

I made a decision to always act in the present moment in a way for which my future self will thank me. *I challenge you to make a list of important events that happened in your life along with what you learned and why you are thankful for these experiences.*

_____

_____

_____

_____

_____

_____

_____

_____

_____

_____

_____

_____

_____

_____

"People rarely succeed unless they have fun in what they are doing."

—*Dale Carnegie*

DECISION #13

Fun

In my early years of life, I would set resolutions at the start of each new year. By March, I would have most likely abandoned them. Sometimes, I would even abandon them by January 2nd. But, I know I wasn't alone because I saw on the news that only about 8% of people actually achieve their New Year's resolutions each year.

As I grew older, I learned about setting S.M.A.R.T. goals. S.M.A.R.T., in its real sense, is the acronym for a lot of realities in the goal setting process. S.M.A.R.T. is known to be the best practice framework for setting goals. To make sure your goals are clear, attainable, and reachable, they must possess the following qualities:

S = Specific

M = Measurable

A = Achievable

R = Relevant

T = Time bound

Learning to set S.M.A.R.T. goals significantly improved my goal setting process and results. However, I also learned there is much more than just setting the right goals.

Only two things set you apart as someone who makes and keeps their resolutions from the rest of people who don't: attitude and belief. In other words, these people think differently. You have to completely change your way of setting resolutions as well as the way you think.

Nowadays, I no longer set New Year's resolutions—I simply set goals.

And if you have goals, you don't need to wait until the beginning of a new year; you can start today because the best time to start something is always yesterday, and the next best time is now. Don't go for perfect—go for done. Speedy action beats perfection any day.

If you've seen the movie *The Secret* and think all you have to do is visualize your dreams and they will come true, then I can confidently tell you it's not completely true, but it's only partially true. Visualizing your dream is just one step in the process of achieving your goals after making the decision. You have to get emotionally involved in your goal and feel the excitement; you have to feel and see yourself achieving the goal. More importantly, you have to experience the joy. In the process, you begin to invoke the Law of Attraction subconsciously which states that what you think about, you bring about. You will begin to attract all that you need to achieve your goal.

A major mistake I see people make when setting goals and New Year's resolutions is using negative words to describe what they want. For example, some people say, "I'm in debt. My goal is to not lose my house." Words are strong. They have energy and power. Negative words produce negative vibrations and, ultimately, negative results. Use positive words instead like this: "I am so happy and grateful now that I have all the money I need to maintain myself in my home and live comfortably." See the difference?

Positive words set up positive vibrations in your body, soul, and mind, helping you begin to attract the people and things you need to achieve your goals. That's why affirmations alone don't work. If you write an affirmation and don't believe it, then you will not be able to make it happen. You will not have the drive to pull through and work towards achieving it.

To change your results, start by changing your words. When the words change, your feelings change and your vibration changes, then your results will change too.

Where people get into trouble is when they try to do this all alone. Everyone can benefit from an objective person to partner with. Having a coach or a mentor can make all the difference in the world. A coach can make this process faster by helping you get clear about what you want and by helping to uncover unconscious motivations which may be sabotaging results. Using a coach can shorten the learning curve and provide support and encouragement throughout the process.

Most importantly, I firmly believe the number one reason why people don't reach their goals is because they are not having enough fun.

In the pursuit of our goals, we often get caught up in the notion that success requires dedication, hard work, and sacrifice. While these characteristics are undoubtedly important, there is one often-overlooked factor which can have a significant impact on your path to success, and that is joy.

When you think about having fun, it can seem irrelevant to achieving your goals. But incorporating joy and carefreeness into our pursuits can change things. I would not have recorded 200 episodes of my podcast if I wasn't having fun and laughing with each guest. This book would never have come to existence if I didn't enjoy opening up my Google Docs.

Having fun has served me as a sustainable source of motivation through slower days and darker times. When you truly enjoy working towards your goals, it becomes much easier to stay active and consistent. Fun infuses our efforts with enthusiasm and passion, and it helps us maintain the drive we need to overcome inevitable challenges and setbacks.

Fun has an amazing ability to unleash our creativity and inspire innovative thinking. When you allow yourself to just play, experiment, and tackle challenges in an easy-going way, you'll see that new perspectives, unconventional solutions, and fresh ideas emerge. Fun fosters creative problem-solving and creates an environment filled with innovation.

Pursuing goals does not mean sacrificing ambition or compromising dedication to enjoy it. It's about adding joy, playfulness, and fulfillment to our journey. By intentionally having more fun in the work we do, we create an environment where goals are a source of inspiration, personal growth, and lasting fulfillment.

So, remember to have more fun. Laugh and enjoy yourself as you work towards your goals. Only when we find ways to make life more fun can we unlock our true potential, find lasting motivation, and pave the way to success and personal fulfillment.

JOURNAL PROMPT #13

I made a decision to prioritize having fun in all that I do. *How can you have more fun while working on your goals?*

_____

_____

_____

_____

_____

_____

_____

_____

_____

_____

_____

_____

_____

"The key to growth is the introduction of higher dimensions of consciousness into our awareness."

—Lao Tzu

DECISION #14
Awareness

It's funny how before I started formally coaching, I didn't even know about life coaching as a career. I was always asked by others how I was so positive, how I did things, or why I didn't need support. People loved the advice I gave, and I realized I have the natural superpower to turn negative thoughts into positive ones.

Then, I also started to realize that one of the most common pieces of advice I offered was to develop more self-awareness. Being unaware of your own problems usually means having limited insight into your own thoughts, feelings, and actions, as well as the impact of these factors on your wellbeing. This lack of confidence can manifest itself in many ways.

For example, if you are unconscious about your problems, you are most likely to repeat the same patterns of behavior or make the same mistakes over and over again without realizing the root cause. Some may blame external circumstances or others for their problems instead of reflecting within themselves. Other people may not be aware of their role or responsibility in dealing with the issues they face. Without awareness, a person may find it difficult to introspect and can find it difficult to examine their thoughts, feelings, and motives and, therefore, lack insight into their experiences.

A lack of awareness can limit our knowledge of our own strengths, weaknesses, values, and personal boundaries. This can make it difficult to make informed decisions or act in line with our personal values.

It is important to note that lack of awareness does not mean a person is inherently flawed or unable to evolve. Self-awareness is developed through self-reflection, seeking feedback, practicing mindfulness, and participating in personal development activities. Through a commitment to self-discovery and growth, anyone can increase their awareness and gain greater insight into themselves and their challenges, paving the way for personal transformation and enhanced wellbeing.

Indeed, I now believe awareness is key to finding solutions to all the problems we face in our lives. It serves as the foundation for developing effective strategies, making fast decisions, and overcoming challenges in a clear and targeted manner.

In essence, awareness is recognizing and acknowledging the existence of a problem. We need a willingness to face the truth, even if it is uncomfortable or difficult to do so. By clarifying current problems, you lay the groundwork for finding solutions and initiating positive change.

As we grow in awareness, we gain a deeper understanding of the root causes, complexity, and impact of our problems. This allows us to analyze various factors and identify the root cause which is the ultimate needle mover of our problems. This level of insight is very important as it allows us to address the core cause of the problem rather than just treating the symptoms or putting a bandage on the situation.

Awareness fosters empathy and understanding to ourselves. It encourages us to think about different perspectives and the potential impact of our actions and decisions on others. This broader awareness helps foster compassion and cooperation, recognizing the interconnectedness of our lives and the importance of working together to find mutually beneficial solutions.

Increased awareness helps us recognize patterns and trends, both in our personal lives and in the world around us. By adjusting these patterns, you can identify recurring problems, anticipate potential issues, and proactively address problems before they escalate. This proactive approach to problem solving helps prevent future escalation and recurrence of problems.

Awareness also fosters curiosity and a mindset of continuous learning. It encourages you to seek knowledge, explore different perspectives, and challenge your own assumptions. This open-mindedness makes you more receptive to innovative ideas and alternative approaches, which ultimately improves your problem-solving skills.

Starting with awareness allows us to approach the problem holistically and strategically. It provides a solid foundation upon which effective solutions can be developed, whether on an individual, community, or global level.

Without awareness, you risk reacting impulsively or applying superficial solutions which fail to address the root cause. So, let's harness the power of consciousness in our lives. We want to face the problem head-on, recognize its existence, and deeply understand its complexity. In doing so, we unlock the potential to create meaningful change, create innovative solutions, and pave the way for a better future.

Self-awareness is the ability to see your life honestly without being fixated on right or wrong, good or bad. Circumstances are neutral, so free yourself from attachments of being right or wrong and simply bring about a higher level of awareness around your problems. With enough practice, you will start to see that many of those problems might be merely "perceived problems."

Let's imagine Anna, who is constantly overwhelmed and stressed about work. She feels too much responsibility, struggles with time management, and often suffers from burnout. But she doesn't take the time to think about the root causes of her stress or the factors contributing to her overwhelming workload.

When Anna becomes more self-aware of her problems, she begins to see patterns in her behavior and emotions. Through introspection, she begins to find it difficult to say "no" to extra work and tends to take on more work than she can handle. She also notices a tendency to prioritize work over her own wellbeing and neglects self-care and personal boundaries.

With this newfound confidence, she can start taking steps to solve the problem. She can start setting boundaries and learn how to say "no" when the workload is too much. To stay healthy, she might prioritize self-care activities such as exercise, mindfulness, and rest. She might also enlist the support of colleagues and managers to delegate tasks and discuss workload concerns. Additionally, self-awareness allows her to review her time management skills, improve efficiency, delegate tasks more effectively, and seek help when needed.

By being proactive in dealing with herself and understanding the causes of her stress, she can take a proactive approach to problem solving. She becomes more attuned to her own needs, recognizes the triggers that contribute to stress, and takes targeted actions to combat them. Over time, her improved confidence has helped her find balance, manage her workload effectively, and create a healthier and more fulfilling work environment.

This example shows how self-awareness can be a powerful catalyst for change, empowering you to identify and understand the underlying factors that contribute to your problems and to develop targeted solutions which address the root causes. Through active self-reflection and self-awareness, you can empower yourself to take responsibility for your challenges and find effective and sustainable solutions. May your journey of awareness lead you to innovative solutions that will positively transform your life and the world around you.

JOURNAL PROMPT #14

I made a decision to bring my consciousness into more awareness in solving all life's problems. *In what areas of your life can you bring a higher level of awareness into?*

_____

_____

_____

_____

_____

_____

_____

_____

_____

_____

_____

_____

_____

_____

_____

"Perfectionism is self-abuse of the highest order."

—*Anne Wilson Schaef*

DECISION #15

Perfectionism

As an ex-perfectionist myself, the topic of how to overcome perfectionism is very keen to my heart. The rise in perfectionism is so troubling that numerous scientific studies found high levels of perfectionism to be correlated with depression, anxiety, eating disorders, self-harm, and a variety of obsessive-compulsive disorders. You might think being a little bit of Ms. Perfect is part of your personality, but let me tell you that everything you ever wanted is on the other side of perfection.

If you are procrastinating, you might be chasing perfection and therefore not taking any action. Perfectionism is often accompanied by hard work and high standards, but it can unintentionally hinder productivity and prevent you from achieving your goals. This can cause unnecessary delays, lost opportunities, and overall inefficiency. In contrast, adopting the "Done is always better than perfect" mindset emphasizes the importance of action and progress.

If you are stressed, you might be thinking an outcome of a circumstance in life is not up to your expectations of perfection. Demanding perfection can lead to overthinking, excessive self-criticism, and holding on to a project until it's perfect.

If you are waiting for when you are good enough, smart enough, or ready enough, then you most likely have fallen into the dark rabbit hole of perfectionism. We must recognize that time is a precious resource and that completing tasks and projects, even if they are not completely perfect, can yield tangible results and drive further growth.

As an ex-perfectionist myself, let me tell you firsthand that perfection is an illusion. It is mission impossible. No matter how hard we strive for perfection, there will always be some amount of error, oversight, or room for improvement. This realization was both humbling and liberating for me.

Perfection often has different meanings for different people. What may be considered perfect by one person may be considered inadequate by another. It is subject to personal biases, cultural norms, and individual perspectives. In many fields, such as art, literature, and music, imperfection is sometimes even celebrated as an expression of individuality and humanity. Recognize that mistakes are an integral part of life and can contribute to a deeper sense of appreciation and connection.

Letting go of perfectionism can help you excel more because contrary to popular belief, perfectionists actually achieve less than those with healthier attitudes because their focus on perfection robs them of motivation and, as I mentioned earlier, brings on procrastination and other negative, self-defeating behaviors.

Well, the good news is that perfectionism can be easily cured by reframing your perfectionistic thoughts. In the last chapter, I talked about how everything starts with awareness. This is also true with overcoming perfectionism. Becoming aware of your tendencies in seeking perfection is the first step to overcoming it.

It is the consistency in your actions, not the perfections in your actions, that will propel you forward. Hence one of my life mottos: "Done is always better than perfect."

This motto embodies the philosophy of prioritizing achievement and progress over the relentless pursuit of perfection. This suggests that it is often more beneficial to complete a task or project, even if it is not performed with utmost perfection, rather than striving endlessly for an unattainable standard of accuracy.

Additionally, the philosophy that "Done is always better than perfect" helps mitigate the devastating effects of perfectionism. It encourages you to overcome your fear of failure as progress and learn to take precedence over the need to be perfect. This mindset promotes a healthier approach to work and reduces stress and burnout by allowing you to focus on what really matters: delivering results and achieving goals.

However, it is important to note that the principle that "Done is always better than perfect" does not encourage sloppy or careless work. It simply encourages you to find a balance between achieving quality results and recognizing that the pursuit of perfection is counterproductive. It promotes perfection as an often unattainable ideal and how progress and achievement should be celebrated and appreciated.

Ultimately, the philosophy that "Done is always better than perfect" emphasizes the importance of taking action, making progress, and completing tasks and projects rather than endlessly chasing an unattainable standard of perfection. By adopting this mindset, you can increase productivity, generate momentum, and experience personal and professional growth. In other words, it is the realization that progress and achievement have inherent value and can lead to tangible results in the pursuit of goals and aspirations.

Instead of constantly feeling disappointed, set more realistic expectations about yourself, others, and the timing you need to finish a project. This approach encourages you to set realistic goals, set achievable milestones, and focus on completing tasks within reasonable timeframes. Cultivate a culture of productivity, innovation, and continuous improvement which focuses on learning from mistakes and implementing ideas rather than clinging to unattainable results.

Instead of criticizing yourself, practice self-compassion. Give yourself grace for all that you have already accomplished. Think about the last time you finished a goal and how amazing you felt when you did. Done is always better than inaction.

The only way to improve at something is to try, fail, and try some more. You are learning along the way, so enjoy the process of learning. Let's make this journey a fun one. Find joy in the process, celebrate progress, and learn from setbacks and mistakes.

Remember this: it is impossible to please everyone around you. Don't compare yourself to others and don't overthink all the possible outcomes. Good is the enemy of great. But perfect is the enemy of everything.

Now repeat after me now:

I am unique, I am limited edition, and I love love love the imperfect me!

JOURNAL PROMPT #15

I made a decision to overcome perfectionism and take pride in taking imperfect actions. *Are you holding back on taking any action because you are waiting for that perfect time? Are you a recovering perfectionist?*

_____

_____

_____

_____

_____

_____

_____

_____

_____

_____

_____

_____

_____

_____

_____

_____

"It's a wise man who understands that every day is a new beginning."

—*Mel Gibson*

DECISION #16
New Day

For much of my twenties, I was on autopilot. I was merely going through the repeated motions of working, sleeping, and waiting for the days to end. Even though I had what many people in society deemed as success, I often felt a deep sense of emptiness and disconnection from the world around me on the inside. My existence felt monotonous, meaningless, and void of passion or fulfillment. I became disinterested in many activities I used to enjoy, had less desire to pursue new experiences, and felt cut off from meaningful relationships. My days were blurred, and my general sense of time passed without much impact or meaning.

My life was shiny on the outside. I only showed beautiful photos on social media when I traveled. I dropped out of sight from my friends, many of whom naturally assumed I had just married off well. But the reality was that I was hustling my butt off. I didn't have any other memories besides sweating myself through paperwork, emails, and meetings. There was a lack of enthusiasm and joy in life, which led me to watch life pass by without much active participation. I was dreading aging, and I was dreading much of each and every day.

As days turned into weeks, months, and years, I began to lose hope, believing my circumstances couldn't be changed and the best days were in the past. I didn't pay any attention to personal growth and self-improvement. The future seemed bleak, and I was ready to settle for living passively, counting the days until the end.

Of course, everyone's experience is different. Maybe you've been there too. Maybe your reasons for living on autopilot were even more complex, stemming from personal circumstances, past trauma, or underlying mental illness. But nevertheless, I've interviewed incredible women who have gone through all types of trials and tribulations and transformed their lives completely. I myself since then have turned my life a complete 180 degrees.

I learned and realized that this state of autopilot was not a permanent punishment. In fact, everything in life is temporary. Even life itself is temporary. With the right support, introspection, and a willingness to embrace changes, we can get out of any dark tunnels and rediscover the meaning, passion, and joy of life. Through incessant learning and personal development, I reclaimed my personal values and gained new experiences to break free from the shackles of life, which ultimately led to a much more fulfilling life.

No matter how hard the past was, no matter what you have been through, no matter who you were with, no matter where you have been, no matter what stories you've been telling yourself, you absolutely can always begin again.

There is always a fresh start. You have the power to hit the reset button any time in life. You can reset your intentions and thoughts any time throughout the day. You have the choice to embrace a new perspective and turn setbacks into comebacks. Adversity to victory, challenge to win, obstacles to success, defeat to revival, hurdles to rebound, depression to prosperity—whatever you want to call it, it is possible.

Every day when you wake up, take a deep breath and smile. You have a new chance to prove yourself. You are given a new chance to follow your dreams. You are given a new day to invest in yourself. Just imagine the compounding effects of yield in your future.

Rather than blaming yourself, others, or even the universe, be aware that tomorrow is another new day and a new opportunity. And what can be more exciting than that? Each day becomes a blank slate, allowing you to face life with renewed determination, optimism, and resilience.

Every day is a chance to begin again. Don't focus on the failures of yesterday. Don't focus on the struggles of your circumstances. Start today with positive thoughts and expectations. It's okay to make mistakes and encounter failures because every day is an opportunity to learn, become stronger, and redefine the way you do things. This encourages us to let go of self-limiting beliefs and negative monologues which can hinder our progress. Instead, embrace a mindset of confidence, resilience, and personal growth. Regardless of past experiences and setbacks, each new day is an opportunity to start over, set new goals, and make choices that align with your ambitions.

Remember when you were young, as a child you'd run and jump and reach to the sky, chasing and popping bubbles. So carefree, free of reservations and constraints, children enjoy the present moment, delighting in their excitement, in the gift of bubbly, soapy play.

This happiness is contagious. It can spread like pollen in the breeze. This is what playful looks like. This is what joyful looks like. We were free back then. And we can be free now too. This serves you as a powerful reminder to embrace the present moment, let go of the past, and face each new day with renewed purpose, determination, and optimism. It encourages us to take responsibility for our lives, make positive choices, and embark on an ongoing journey of personal growth and fulfillment.

It doesn't matter what your present circumstances look like; today is a brand-new day! The best time to do something was always yesterday, and the next best time is today. Today is the day! Today is the day you get to make that decision. Today is the day you can let it go. Today is the day you decide to rise. Today is the day you intentionally leave behind what's not serving you.

Life is miraculous because every day is a new beginning. So, if you are alive and with me right now, let's do something remarkable. Go after your dreams! Live your life the way you want to live! You can, and you will! You are remarkable—always remember that!

JOURNAL PROMPT #16

I made a decision that every day can be a new beginning, and it is never too late to pivot or reach for those secret dreams. *Do you have a secret dream from childhood buried deep in your heart? Do you have a plan that's been put on the backburner?*

_____

_____

_____

_____

_____

_____

_____

_____

_____

_____

_____

_____

_____

"Stress acts as an accelerator: it will push you either forward or backward, but you choose which direction."

—*Chelsea Erieau*

DECISION #17

Stress

As a life coach, one question I get asked often is how I deal with everyday stress and cope with my busy workdays. My answer is that my workdays are never too busy. It is much easier to prevent stress than it is to deal with stress. I teach my clients how to better manage their time, so they set realistic goals, focus on the simple joys of life, and never have to feel there is too much on their plate. We rid the word overwhelm by attending our own non-negotiable activities first and understanding our values and priorities. This way, you can crush your goals with clarity, not with burnout.

Yes, stress is an inevitable part of life. I don't know anyone who has never experienced stress. But, instead of simply accepting stress as an inevitable part of our existence, we can shift our perspective and take a positive attitude to prevent stress altogether. The time has come to prioritize our peace, happiness, and joy.

Stress is like a guest who lingers longer than welcomed. It creeps into our lives and drains our energy, dulling our minds and reducing our sense of wellbeing. But what if we could take responsibility and prevent stress from crashing uninvited?

Imagine a life where you are not under constant stress. You can control your emotions, and you can easily overcome difficulties. It's within your reach, my friend. By prioritizing stress prevention, you can build a life of balance, resilience, and peace of mind.

Stress prevention begins with self-care. We need to recognize that our mental, emotional, and physical health deserve our utmost attention. It is not selfish. It is not selfish. It is not selfish. I need to say this three times to emphasize its importance. It is necessary for our overall wellbeing and success. By investing time and effort in self-care, we can combat stress.

Cultivate mindfulness in your daily life. Enjoy the simple pleasures, let go of worries about the past or the future, and be fully present in the current moment. Practicing mindfulness helps us face challenges with clarity and calmness, without surrendering to the chaos of stress.

Take control of your schedule. Set boundaries and learn to say "no" when necessary. Overcommitment and endless to-do lists can lead to overwhelming stress. Prioritize your tasks, delegate them when possible, and set aside space for rest and relaxation. Maintain healthy relationships and surround yourself with a supportive network. Connection and belonging are powerful buffers against stress. Lean on your loved ones, share their burdens, and offer support in return. Together, we can face any challenge with strength and resilience.

Do you play sports regularly? Exercise not only strengthens our bodies, but it also releases natural mood-boosting endorphins which fight stress. Find an activity that brings you joy, like dancing, hiking, or yoga. Make exercise a source of stress prevention and refreshment. Make a list of all the activities that bring you joy.

Harness the power of positivity. Cultivate optimism and gratitude. Focus on what you can control and let go of what you can't reach. Practice redefining challenges as opportunities for growth and learning. By changing your perspective, you can turn stress into a catalyst for self-growth.

Remember: prevention is always better than cure. By actively preventing stress, we regain our peace of mind and wellbeing. We create lives of resilience, balance, and joy. I encourage you to take steps to prevent stress. This includes prioritizing self-care, cultivating mindfulness, being social, engaging in physical activity, and developing a positive attitude. Together, let's build a life filled with peace of mind, resilience, and freedom from stress. May your stress prevention efforts lead you to a happy and fulfilling life.

Nevertheless, sometimes life throws us curve balls, and circumstances arise that cause stress. In these moments, it is time to think of stress as a powerful force that has the potential to change the course of our lives. Think of it not as a problem but as an accelerator which drives us forward or backward depending on the choices we make accordingly. In this analogy, we are the drivers, and stress drives our journey. The direction we take is ultimately determined by the way we think, our resilience, and our ability to meet the challenges posed by stress.

Let stress be a catalyst for growth and drive you to success and personal development. When faced with stressful situations, you have options. You can give in to the pressure and allow it to push you back, or you can use it as an opportunity to grow and move forward.

In the face of stress, instead of being overwhelmed, see the stress as a cue to dig deeper, adjust your strategies, and move forward with unwavering determination. By reframing stress in this way, you tap into your inner resilience and find creative solutions to overcome challenges. The key difference lies in the choices we make when faced with stress. The direction we take ultimately determines the outcome of our journey.

So, when stress comes into your life, accept it as your driving force. Realize that it is your choices, your mindset, and your resilience which determine whether you move forward or backward. Use stress as an opportunity for growth and harness your inner strength to bring you success and personal fulfillment.

Remember, you are the driver of your own life. Choose a path that leads to a future filled with growth, resilience, and limitless possibilities. May your decisions in the face of stress always propel you on the path to success.

JOURNAL PROMPT #17

I made a decision to prioritize my wellbeing in order to prevent stress, so I don't have to deal with stress. *What immediate actions can you take now to prevent stress?*

_____

_____

_____

_____

_____

_____

_____

_____

_____

_____

_____

_____

_____

_____

"To forgive is to set a prisoner free and discover that the prisoner was you."

—*Lewis B. Smedes*

DECISION #18

Forgive

I've always considered myself to be a forgiving person. I accepted apologies with a warm, open heart and prided myself in being "nice." I always reminded myself to try to understand and share the emotions of others—to be empathetic. I tried hard to think of myself in someone else's shoes and see things from their point of view. But as I grew older, I realized that I'm much "nicer" to others than I am to myself.

I found it difficult to forgive myself for past mistakes, such as wrong decisions, harmful actions, or decisions which have had negative consequences for myself or others. Holding on to these feelings put a huge dent in my self-esteem.

I hated myself when I accidentally hurt others' feelings and also hated myself for letting others hurt my feelings. I would think about and regret missed opportunities, which led to difficulties in self-accountability and self-forgiveness. I set super high standards for myself and sometimes found it difficult to forgive myself for not recognizing mistakes or failing to meet my own expectations. When I acted against my core values and principles, I found it difficult to forgive myself for damaging my own integrity. When I neglected my responsibilities and obligations to myself and others, such as not keeping promises and commitments, I found it difficult to forgive myself.

And worst of all was the negative self-talks, self-doubts, and feelings of worthlessness which all made it even more difficult to forgive myself. Internalizing criticism created obstacles to self-forgiveness. I would never say some of the hurtful things I've said to myself to others.

Through my personal development journey, I learned that self-forgiveness is a very personal and complex process. It requires introspection, acceptance, and compassion. But I knew that both forgiving myself and others is imperative to my life.

Practicing forgiveness can have powerful health and wellbeing benefits. Many studies suggest that forgiveness is associated with lower levels of depression, anxiety, and depression, reduced substance abuse, higher self-esteem, healthier relationships, stronger immune systems, and greater life satisfaction overall.

Some may think that forgiving is a sign of weakness and giving power to someone else; however, forgiveness is incredibly powerful for yourself because it is all about owning your personal power. Forgiveness is giving yourself the opportunity to learn, to grow, and to heal. Forgiveness means giving up the suffering of the past and being willing to forge ahead with inner freedom to live your life to a higher potential.

We can even find that past negative experiences are usually blessings in disguise if we can create the place for forgiveness and true acceptance in our hearts. I'm here to remind you that forgiveness is your own responsibility. It has nothing to do with another person or who you are forgiving or who needs to forgive you. Only you can unlock the door to your own prison and shift your life from your self-imposed limitations to true freedom. Only you can take your power back and focus on your own desires instead of taking revenge or living in the past.

Create an action plan on how to shift your resentful thoughts when negative feelings come up. Even once you forgive, some old mental patterns may still come back or be triggered. Write down your affirmations or manifestos of what you will say to remind yourself of your forgiveness and shift your focus back to your true desires.

The secret to forgiveness is to release all your expectations from anyone else. This includes expectations of forgiveness or apologies from others or changes in other people's behaviors.

Now to make things clear, forgiving doesn't mean accepting unacceptable behavior. If the person does not change, then it is your responsibility to do what's right for you. However, by the act of forgiving and experiencing the power of forgiveness, you can regain your power and move on to what matters most in life to you.

Forgiveness is a powerful and transformative act, and it can have profound effects on both the forgiving and the forgiven. Forgiveness has the power to heal wounds and promote peace of mind. By letting go of anger, resentment, and bitterness, forgiveness allows you to let go of the emotional burden that weighs on you. When you choose to forgive, you feel a sense of relief, and the physiological and psychological effects of stress are reduced.

Forgiveness repairs and strengthens relationships. It opens the door to reconciliation, communication, and understanding. By forgiving others, you develop empathy, compassion, and a willingness to deal with conflict. This creates healthier and more fulfilling connections with others.

Forgiveness is an act of personal growth and recovery. It requires you to face your pain, face your emotions, and intentionally choose a healing path. Forgiveness frees you from attachment to the past. In doing so, you can free yourself from the negative experiences, mistakes, and pain which might be holding you back from reaching your highest potential. Through forgiveness, you regain your power and the ability to focus on the present moment and incredible future possibilities.

Don't forgive because of any other reason than wanting to live your life with freedom and passion. Forgive because you value your desires and you want to live life on your own terms from now on.

JOURNAL PROMPT #18

I made a decision to always forgive myself and others. *I challenge you now to make a list of people you need to forgive and what you want to forgive them for. Even more importantly, this can also include what you need to forgive yourself for. Don't hold on to any negative feelings about yourself. If you feel you have made some bad decisions or mistakes in the past, forgive yourself. From failed relationships to weakness, from people you have judged to losing your hopes and dreams, it's never too late to forgive and reset your life.*

_____

_____

_____

_____

_____

_____

_____

_____

_____

_____

"We cannot solve our problems with the same level of thinking that created them."

—*Albert Einstein*

DECISION #19

Overthinking

If you ever find yourself thinking about why you overthink everything or suffer from ruminating thoughts, then you are not alone. I am a recovering overthinker and on my own journey to recovering from overthinking. I fell in love with helping others overcome overthinking.

By definition, overthinking is to think about something too much or for too long. But what's even worse? Spending more time thinking about if you are overthinking or why you are overthinking in the first place. Then, we begin to make up problems that don't even exist. If you consistently focus on ruminating and making it a habit, it becomes a loop. And the more you do it, the harder it is to stop this loop. Many times, overthinking is a very sneaky form of fear as it can be much less obvious than fear.

Of course, we don't want to make snap decisions in life without research, but we don't want to overthink either. Why do we need to stop overthinking on the spot? Because at the very the least, it steals your happiness, creativity, time, and goals. It's very normal to have some tendencies to overthink, and as long as we are aware, we can change the narrative and stop overthinking. But if we don't stop overthinking, in serious cases, it can lead to many mental health issues like depression, anxiety, post-traumatic stress, or even borderline personality disorder.

The specific circumstances that cause overthinking vary from person to person, but it's important to address this topic because overthinking occurs during common daily activities.

For example, have you ever reconsidered your interactions with others and worried about how your actions were received or whether or not you said the right thing? Then, you replay the conversation in your head, analyzing every word and gesture and often questioning yourself. Relationships, whether romantic, familial, or platonic, can be a major source of overthinking. You may analyze conversations that question the intentions and feelings of others and constantly seek validation in your relationships.

Or have you ever cared too much about your appearance? How you dressed, your hairstyle, or body image choices, constantly questioning your attractiveness and comparing yourself to others?

You can overthink things, especially when making important decisions. You may ponder all possible outcomes, repeatedly weighing the pros and cons and being fearful of making the wrong choice. This can lead to a state of analysis paralysis where you overthink and find it difficult to act.

Looking back on past events and regrets can also lead to overthinking. You may repeatedly recall past mistakes, missed opportunities, or embarrassing moments in your mind, which can lead to feelings of guilt, shame, and regret.

Predicting the future also leads to overthinking. You may worry about potential problems, uncertainties, or negative outcomes. Trying to control the unpredictable aspects of life, you may over-plan or ruminate about what might happen.

But even more often, we think too much about our progress toward personal goals and our overall sense of accomplishment. We may compare themselves to others, doubt our own abilities, and fear not meeting the expectations of ourselves and society. Even the most powerful women sometimes temporarily forget our power and start to overthink.

Overthinkers usually focus on details and strive to perfect their actions and surroundings. Worrying too much about doing everything right can lead to increased anxiety and the pressure you put on yourself.

I've been in all of these places myself, and I've seen overthinking in one way or another with all my clients. That is how common overthinking is. But developing strategies to manage and redirect overthinking, such as mindfulness, self-compassion, and seeking support when you need it, can help you find balance and reduce unnecessary stress.

So, how can we stop overthinking? This is what I did, and you can take the same approach. I made a firm and committed decision to stop overthinking. I am a self-proclaimed recovering overthinker. I sometimes also call myself an ex-overthinker. I've decided that overthinking is no longer a part of my present life.

I started to have more awareness when I get stuck in my own head. Overthinking can become such a habit that you don't even recognize when you're doing it most of the time. However, if you are conscious and committed to this change, I promise you will start to catch yourself when it happens.

As I understood the value of "what you focus on grows," I learned to switch my focus. Keep your focus on problem-solving instead of the problem itself. Our perception of things is our own narrative in our heads, and the good news is that narratives can be changed. So when you notice that you're overthinking, challenge them and change them to positive, abundant thoughts.

All skills in life are muscles to be worked on. If you need more mindfulness in your life, then practice yoga, meditation, breathwork, or whatever modality you find most helpful to gain muscle in that area you need to improve.

I encourage you to schedule time for thinking and self-reflection, but only for the type of thinking that is beneficial to reflect. Reflect on how far you have come, how much you have already accomplished, what you have learned, and how you can improve yourself. Reflect on how remarkable you are and how much you have accomplished. Reflection is meant to help you move forward, not to stop you on your tracks. I love this quote by Will Rogers that says, "Even if you are on the right track, you'll get run over if you just stand there."

If you are healthy, you are free to dream hundreds of dreams. When you are unhealthy, you can only have one dream and that is to be healthy again. So, if you are here reading this book, take action towards your dreams and stop overthinking.

JOURNAL PROMPT #19

I made a decision to stop overthinking. *Think of the first goal that comes to mind which you have been overthinking about and take one immediate action today towards that goal.*

_____

_____

_____

_____

_____

_____

_____

_____

_____

_____

_____

_____

"Some of our important choices have a timeline. If we delay a decision, the opportunity is gone forever. Sometimes our doubts keep us from making a choice that involves change. Thus an opportunity may be missed."

—*James E. Faust*

DECISION #20

Decisions

Decision making is a very complex task. It requires time and energy to weigh your options, so many people feel indecisive and suffer from self-doubt which are normal parts of the decision process. In many ways, they're a good thing; they are a sign that you're thinking about your choices instead of just going with the flow. However, you don't want to think about the choices so much that you overthink and fail to make the decision at all. But learning to make fast decisions is an essential part of living a better life.

Of course, there is a mental disorder in which you display pathological indecisiveness and can seek help, or else, you can learn the tools and skills to make faster decisions and know that many times indecisiveness is simply a combination of mindset blocks and anxiety.

Quick decision making helps you complete tasks more efficiently and reach your goals. This helps you to avoid analysis paralysis and overthinking, enabling you to act quickly and move your plans forward. This allows us to seize opportunities, react better to changes, and adapt to new situations with ease. You'll also be better able to think spontaneously, relying more heavily on intuition and experience. This improves your ability to quickly identify problems, evaluate possible solutions, and select the best course of action when time is pressed.

Furthermore, quick decision making allows you to be more agile and flexible, enabling you to change direction or adjust your strategy as needed. This is especially useful in dynamic and unpredictable environments. You can identify potential risks early, assess them efficiently, and take appropriate actions to mitigate or effectively manage them.

Once you are more confident in your decision-making skills, it brings a sense of control, progress, and completion to your life, which helps reduce negative feelings and stress. We have these mindset blocks and anxieties because we as humans, in most cases at least, fear we might make the wrong decision, so we hesitate when we are presented with a choice. Maybe you are afraid of failure, suffering any consequences, or even the consequences of success. Maybe you are worried about what other people will think about you. In many cases, this also ties to perfectionism, and if you feel you are in any way a perfectionist, then you probably struggle greatly with decision making. But I'm here to tell you today the good news: decision making is just another muscle we can build. You can practice being decisive and making faster decisions.

Start to build that decision-making muscle by setting some rules. For example, on social media, my rule is that I do not accept any friendship requests from unknown males. This way, I can easily reject hundreds of such requests at a time without the need to think about it. My rule for family time is that I don't take client calls on weekends, so I have plenty of time for my family, and it's a no-brainer decision when I'm asked for a call on the weekend for any reason. This decision of "no thank you" will be immediate. I know my values, priorities, and boundaries, so when it comes to decision making in those areas, my decisions are always immediate.

Then, you strengthen this muscle by practicing with the small stuff. Set a time for making decisions. For example, give yourself 30 seconds to decide what you'll have for lunch, what movie to watch, or whether you want to go out or not. Follow through on those small decisions and repeat. This is important because it helps you avoid decision-making fatigue. This is why many successful businessmen wear the same thing every day because they don't want to waste time making these small decisions. This is also part of my reason for becoming a vegetarian. I used to be stressed about what to eat all the time. As a vegetarian, restaurants help me make those decisions because usually there are only one or two choices on the menu. And most importantly, making small decisions quickly trains our brains to think through questions faster. Then, you are ready to work up to bigger things.

When making a bigger decision, give yourself a deadline to weigh the different options. If you can't seem to make the decision, turn it around and reverse engineer. Instead of weighing what you will gain from making the decision, think about what you will lose by choosing each option and compare how you will feel losing those options. Ask yourself:

Is this decision healthy?

Is it in alignment with my values, priorities, and goals?

Is it rewarding?

No one makes perfect decisions all the time. Most of us have exes, most of us have been in a job we didn't like, or we have ordered the wrong dish at some point. But hey, action works in our favor, while inaction never does. When you delay decision making because you're afraid of messing up, nothing changes. But when you're proactive, you're choosing to move ahead— and that's one of the best decisions you can ever make.

Always remember this: only action will lead to clarity. I say that repeatedly because it's extremely important. If action leads to clarity, then stop waiting for clarity to take action. You are always making the best decision according to your best knowledge. And if you ever take a wrong turn on the road, just enjoy the different scenery and have fun along the way. Cheers to you for making healthy, successful, and rewarding decisions.

JOURNAL PROMPT #20

I made a decision to always make fast decisions. *Make a list of rules regarding money, life, and social media so that these rules can help you make faster decisions in the future.*

_____

_____

_____

_____

_____

_____

_____

_____

_____

_____

_____

_____

"Remembering that I'll be dead soon is the most important tool I've ever encountered to help me make the big choices in life. Because almost everything – all external expectations, all pride, all fear of embarrassment or failure – these things just fall away in the face of death, leaving only what is truly important."

—*Steve Jobs*

DECISION #21

Bold Moves

Growing up, I never thought of myself as a person who made bold moves. I prided myself in being the top honors student as I valued and excelled in academics. I wanted to be the "good girl" to my parents and society. I followed rules, norms, and traditions while striving to maintain a positive image within my family and community. I was as polite, respectful, and considerate of others as I possibly could be. People around me saw me being responsible and dependable, and they expected me to take my promises seriously—to honor them and to keep them. At work, I was cooperative and obedient, and I avoided behaviors which might be considered provocative or attention-grabbing. I also valued my own honesty, integrity, and sense of right and wrong.

After starting my podcast, I began to share the stories of my life on other podcasts. The most common reaction I received was: "Wow, you made some bold moves!" Really? These reactions were surprising and interesting to me because it was only then I realized it was the bold moves which shaped who I am today and led me to living the best life I now live by design. It's fascinating and enlightening when others recognize and appreciate the courageous steps you've taken in life. These reactions can be recognition and validation of how bold decisions have shaped who you are today and the positive results you achieved because of them.

By sharing my life stories through my podcast, I can give others insight into the choices I made which might seem to be deviated from the norm. These choices may seem daring to some, but they have helped me consciously shape the life I am currently living to suit my tastes and desires. And I want that for you too—for you to live the epic life you deserve by taking actions that are scary or a deviation of what others call normal.

Bold actions often involve stepping out of your comfort zone, taking risks, and challenging societal norms and expectations. By taking these steps, you have demonstrated your willingness to pursue your passions, embrace change, and live a life consistent with who you really are. I encourage you to do so because your willingness to share your stories highlights the transformative power of your bold choices and will encourage others to reflect on their lives and consider the possibilities beyond the traditional path.

These responses to my bold moves served as a reminder of my personal growth and the resilience I have developed. It takes courage to step into an unknown world and make choices that differ from society's expectations. Through these experiences, I have developed self-awareness, confidence, and the ability to deal with uncertainty. This is a testament to inner strength and determination.

Recognizing the role bold actions have played in my life now motivates me to continue taking risks and pursuing opportunities for growth. As I share my stories, my hope is for those of you seeking inspiration to develop the courage to take bold steps. I urge you to think of your own way for making bold moves and tap into possibilities beyond the reach of conventional choices.

If you are thinking of making a bold move, just be ready to experience symptoms of anxiety. You are supposed to get anxious. Every time. If you're not anxious before doing something nerve-racking, then something is wrong. But never limit your confidence levels just because of these temporary emotions.

Set boundaries about how you speak to yourself. Don't say negative things like, "I have low self-esteem," "I can't do it," or "I have anxiety." Instead, say positive things like, "What will I learn from this?" or "I am a little nervous because I'm excited for this."

See yourself as courageous. Honor your own courage and bravery as a choice. Let your decision align with who you want to be and where you want to go. Courage is not the result of letting go and blindly trusting a process. It is the result of understanding and controlling the details of the process. Know what you are getting yourself into, research your options, and understand what is expected.

Focus on small details and routine tasks. The key is that all big, complex problems can be chunked down into small, simple problems. In other words, big audacious goals can be chunked down into smaller pieces. Ask yourself what else you still need to learn to make the move easier. Listen to that podcast, read that book, buy that course, or work with that coach.

Imagine a life where fear does not hold you back—where you can break free from the ordinary and embrace the extraordinary. It is within your reach, waiting for you to take a leap of faith. The truth is that bold action is the catalyst for change, growth, and unprecedented success.

We are all born with dreams and aspirations that whisper to us in our quietest moments. But dreams don't come true just by wishing. It takes drive, courage, and boldness to challenge the status quo. It's time to move beyond the ordinary and into the realm of the extraordinary. Taking bold steps requires facing your fears head-on. It may be temporarily scary, uncomfortable, and unsafe, but in those moments of anxiety lies the true core of personal growth.

Think about some of history's greatest minds, pioneers, and visionaries. They didn't play it safe to achieve great things. They took risks, rebelled against convention, and went their own way. The world rewards those who dare to be different, who have the courage to challenge standards and strive for excellence.

Today, I challenge you to listen to your inner voice—the voice that yearns for more. Believe in your skills, passion, and resilience. A bold step is not just for personal gain. It's important to create a ripple effect which encourages others to do the same. Your boldness is contagious and will bring courage and inspiration to those around you. By taking this step, you can be the lighthouse and show others that they have the power to follow their dreams too.

Remember: life is too short to live in the shadow of doubt and hesitation. Because through these bold steps, we create a world filled with extraordinary people who dream, act, and have the courage to live life to the fullest. May your courage pave the way for a future full of possibilities. Now is the time to live your epic life true to your passions and goals. Let's take a bold step together.

JOURNAL PROMPT #21

I made a decision to make bold moves in life. *If nothing is in your way—money, time, and all other excuses are not considered— what is one bold move you would like to make in life?*

_____

_____

_____

_____

_____

_____

_____

_____

_____

_____

_____

_____

_____

ACKNOWLEDGEMENTS

I have to start by thanking my awesome parents, or else I wouldn't be here. You always make me feel safe and loved. Thank you so much; I love you dearly.

Writing a book took longer than I thought, but it was more rewarding than I could have ever imagined. None of this would have been possible without my husband's and daughter's support. Thank you; I love you both to the moon and back.

I appreciate you so much, Sydney Owens. You are truly the best editor heaven sent.

This book was two years in the making and on the back burner until I invested in Gabby Berstein's Bestseller Masterclass which helped me outline the entire book in just one sitting. Thank you, Gabby, for your book writing process and incredible guided meditations.

Thank you, Dino Gomez, for giving me the light bulb to this book title; I appreciate you and the entire 7 Figure Visionary Mastermind crew.

Although my life was filled with many ups and downs, it is so much more fun with you in it, my dear friend Zoe Zhang. Thank you for your friendship and beautiful design of the front book cover.

I'm eternally blessed to have two amazing souls in my life who share the same birthdays as me—yes, we were born on the same day, month, and year. To Nancy Chien and Yan Jiang, your sisterhood and friendship is something beyond magical; no matter how far apart we are in distance, we are always close in the heart.

Thank you, Natalie Bacon. You were the only blogger I followed way back in the day, and I am so incredibly thankful the universe brought you into the coaching world and helped me find you.

Please give a round of applause to Amanda Perna, who dressed me for the book cover and inspires me in so many ways.

How incredibly talented is the amazing Molly McCauley for capturing the perfect shot of me for the book cover at The Altitude Summit. Your photography skills amaze me beyond words.

Thank you, Jess Ekstrom; your Bookpop Workshop gave me the extra confidence boost I needed to complete this project. I'm so grateful for the MicDrop speaker sisterhood community you created, and I thank you for your vision to put more women speakers on stage.

A very special thanks to Sheena Yap Chan. Thank you for opening the podcasting door for me, to which I fell madly in love with and found profound fulfillment in bringing uplifting content into the world.

Thank you, Amy Edge, for starting the movement of Rising Sisterhood. I'm honored to have been in the inaugural group and to be a co-author on the first book. You taught me about the self-publishing path, and I'm forever grateful.

Thank you, Tam Luc, for inviting me to be a co-author in Asian Women Who Bossup book. This opportunity ignited a deeper passion in me for book writing.

Thank you to all my amazing guests who have been interviewed on The Lucy Liu Show; it's been an honor to speak with you and learn from all of you remarkable women.

I'm also beyond grateful for my incredible clients; I appreciate you all for having trusted me in your uprising journeys. Thank you for trusting me as your guide to your next level, and you also inspire me.

Finally, to you, thank you for reading this book. Keep being remarkable, and may all kinds of blessings continue to shower your life!

ABOUT THE AUTHOR

Lucy Liu is a master life coach helping women uplevel in business and life to confidently live an epic life! She is an unshakable optimist, wife, mom, entrepreneur, empowerment workshop facilitator, motivational speaker, best-selling author, and podcast host of The Lucy Liu Show.

Entrepreneurs and high achievers hire her to see clarity and take quantum leaps FAST because most of them are overthinking, scattered, and self-doubting. She's best at helping you get unstuck, make faster decisions, and fulfill higher potential. Bottom line: you can not only make more money and have a greater impact, but you can also have more fun and live an EPIC life by design.

When she's not podcasting, speaking, or coaching, she is either working on her next book in her Los Angeles home or traveling around the world.

Connect with Lucy:
Website: www.lucyliucoaching.com
Instagram: www.instagram.com/mslucyliu
LinkedIn: www.linkedin.com/in/mslucyliu
Facebook: www.facebook.com/mslucyliu
Twitter: www.twitter.com/mslucyliu
TikTok: https://www.tiktok.com/@mslucyliu
YouTube: https://www.youtube.com/@mslucyliu
Podcast: www.lucyliucoaching.com/podcast

www.ingramcontent.com/pod-product-compliance
Lightning Source LLC
Chambersburg PA
CBHW060432090426
42733CB00011B/2249